Vietnam *1939–75*

NEIL DEMARCO

Contents

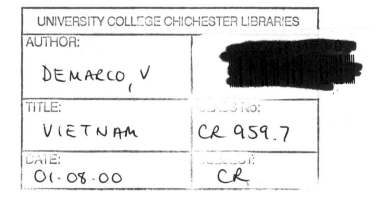

Hodder & Stoughton
A MEMBER OF THE HODDER HEADLINE GROUP

1

Vietnam During the Second World War

Key Issue **How did the war affect Vietnam?**

In 1939 Vietnam was part of an area known as French Indo-China. French Indo-China consisted of Vietnam, Laos and Cambodia. The French had added these areas to their **empire** in the 19th century. French Indo-China had a population of 25 million, of which 20 million lived in Vietnam. The French ruled Vietnam directly but the royal families of Laos and Cambodia ruled in these areas under overall French control.

Indo-China was rich in natural resources. It was the world's third largest grower of rice. It also had corn, coal and rubber. This made it a valuable area to control. After France's defeat by the Germans in June 1940 it became very difficult for the French to keep control of Indo-China. Some Vietnamese saw France's defeat as an opportunity for independence. France's chances of keeping control were not improved by the presence of Japan in the area.

Japanese ambitions

Japan was keen to extend its influence in South East Asia in order to gain control of vital raw materials, such as those mentioned above. France's defeat in Europe gave Japan its chance to move in on Indo-China.

What made Japan's interest in Indo-China more urgent was the fact that the Japanese had been at war with China since 1937. The Chinese had been receiving supplies by rail from Haiphong in Vietnam.

The Japanese demanded that the French close down the railway and in September 1940 Japanese troops occupied Haiphong. By this time France was partly under German occupation. The southern part of France, called **Vichy** France, became a neutral state under German 'influence'. Vichy France still had control over French **colonies** but it wasn't in a position to resist Japanese aggression. The Vichy government accepted the occupation of Haiphong and northern Vietnam – despite the fact that 800 French troops had been killed in the attack.

Indo-China occupied

In July 1941 Vichy France agreed to allow the Japanese to occupy the rest of French Indo-China. The official reason given by the Vichy French was that the British were plotting against French rule in Indo-China and the Japanese were merely protecting it. The real reason was that France could not defend its colony against a Japanese army of 35 000 and had no choice. The Japanese allowed the French to continue running Indo-China

A French Indo-China was a long way from France and difficult to defend against an aggressive power like Japan. The Japanese also forced France to hand over territory to Siam in 1941. Siam later became an ally of Japan. (Siam became Thailand in 1949.)

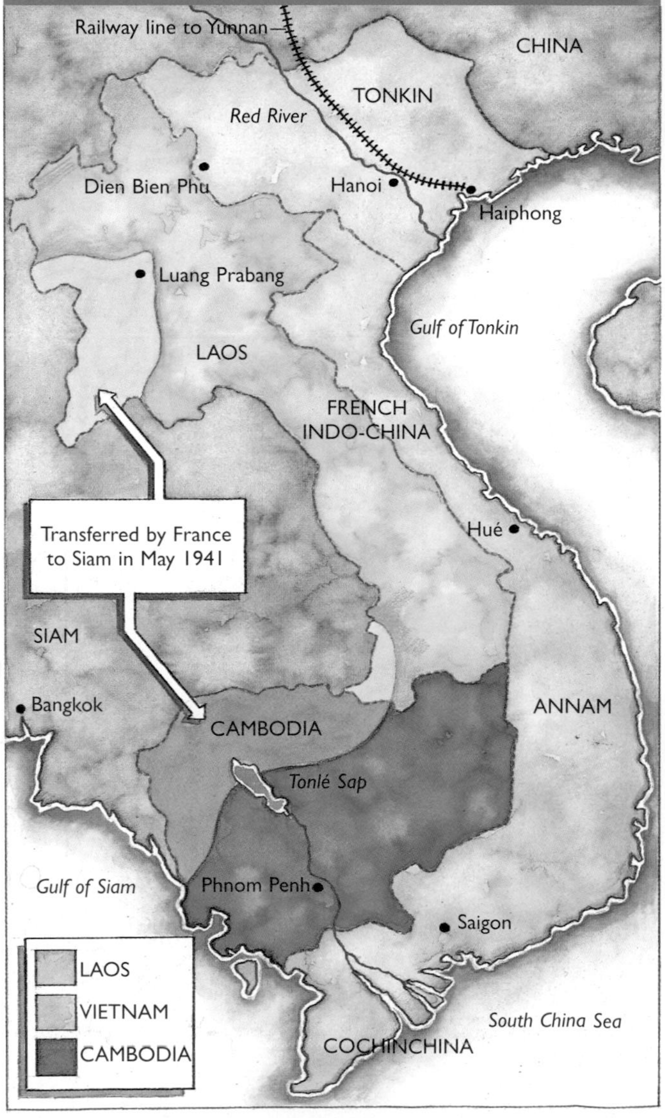

Railway line to Yunnan
CHINA
TONKIN
Red River
Dien Bien Phu
Hanoi
Haiphong
Luang Prabang
Gulf of Tonkin
LAOS
FRENCH INDO-CHINA
Transferred by France to Siam in May 1941
Hué
SIAM
Bangkok
ANNAM
CAMBODIA
Tonlé Sap
Gulf of Siam
Phnom Penh
Saigon
LAOS
VIETNAM
CAMBODIA
South China Sea
COCHINCHINA

as long as the Japanese could take whatever resources they needed for their war against China.

The Japanese ruthlessly stripped all that they could from the region. The effect was that the local population starved. Between one and a half and two million Vietnamese starved to death in 1945. But the Vietnamese did not need to wait for an event like this to organise resistance to the Japanese.

The Vietminh

In 1941 two leading Vietnamese **communists**, Ho Chi Minh and Nguyen Vo Giap (a history teacher), set up the League for the Independence of Vietnam (or Vietminh) in southern China. Though Ho Chi Minh and Giap were communists, the Vietminh included non-communist organisations as well. The aim of the Vietminh was essentially a **nationalist** one: to establish an independent Vietnam, free from foreign domination. This meant fighting both the Japanese and the French.

The Communist Party of Vietnam was founded in 1930 in southern China.

Ho Chi Minh

Ho was born in 1890 and was the son of a peasant. He became a school teacher but left Vietnam for Europe in 1911 as kitchen boy on a French ship. He worked as a pastry cook in a London hotel and began to get interested in politics. He then spent six years in Paris. Ho was strongly opposed to French rule in his country but he admired French culture.

B Ho Chi Minh (centre) was an impressive leader. He led a simple, modest life and had a strong personality. He also had a shrewd grasp of politics. He realised that the Vietminh would attract less support if it was only a communist organisation. Ho, therefore, played down his communist beliefs.

He soon became a communist because communist Russia promised to assist all peoples struggling to free themselves from foreign rule. 'It was patriotism and not communism that originally inspired me' he later said. In 1929 he founded the Indo-Chinese Communist Party.

The Vietminh was still operating from China. But it also had the help of the American intelligence service, the Organisation of Strategic Services (OSS). The OSS trained and equipped the Vietminh during the war. By the end of 1944 the Vietminh were ready to begin **guerrilla** operations against the Japanese and French in northern Vietnam.

Their campaign was mostly small-scale attacks against isolated French outposts but they were successful. Support for the Vietminh grew as a result and by early 1945 the Vietminh had about 5000 guerrilla fighters under the command of Giap.

The defeat of Japan

The Japanese tried hard to hold on to Vietnam and in March 1945 they decided to get rid of the French altogether. French troops were disarmed or killed and French officials imprisoned. The Japanese offered to set up an independent Vietnam, totally free from French control. They appointed Bao Dai, the Emperor of Vietnam since 1925, as its leader.

But it was a pointless move. In August 1945 the Japanese surrendered and the Second World War was over. The Japanese would have to withdraw from all the countries of South East Asia under their control. The question was: who would replace the Japanese in Vietnam? Ho was determined that it would be the Vietminh and not the French.

Q

1 What regions made up Indo-China?
2 Why were the Japanese so keen to control Indo-China?
3 Why did the Vietminh attract the support of many Vietnamese?
4 a) What do you suppose Ho meant when he said 'It was patriotism and not communism that originally inspired me'?
   b) Why do you think he said this?
5 Why did the defeat of Japan in 1945 achieve only one of the aims of the Vietminh?

The War Against the French

Why were the French defeated?

The Vietminh were quick to replace the French and Japanese. They took control of Hanoi and Saigon and in September 1945 Ho announced that Vietnam was an independent and democratic republic. The United States was sympathetic. The Americans didn't want to see the old colonial powers like France back in charge. They believed that the Vietnamese and other Asian peoples had the right to rule themselves.

The French return

By December 1945 there were 50 000 French troops in Indo-China ready to complete the task of restoring French power there. The Vietminh were not strong in the south of Vietnam and the French commander, Leclerc, claimed victory by March 1946.

In fact, Leclerc had made the classic mistake of professional soldiers fighting an enemy which used guerrilla tactics. The French could conquer Vietminh territory but they could not keep control of it. As soon as they moved on, the Vietminh would return to the villages. Leclerc simply did not have enough troops to hold down the areas they captured. The Americans were to face the same problem 20 years later. As one Vietminh fighter said of this time, 'We couldn't protect the villages, the French couldn't hold them.'

For a while an uneasy truce existed between the French in the south and Ho Chi Minh in the north. Ho travelled to Paris to work out an agreement but negotiations broke down. Both sides could only agree on a ceasefire.

In November 1946 the French broke the ceasefire and launched a major attack against the Vietminh forces in Haiphong. The following month fighting started in Hanoi as well. The Vietminh retreated into the jungle, 100 kilometres north of Hanoi, and prepared for guerrilla war. They were heavily outnumbered to begin with and there was little fighting until 1950. The important development in this time was political and not military.

By 1950 the Americans' attitude to French rule in Vietnam had completely changed. The **Cold War** with the Soviet Union meant that the United States would now assist any country opposing the

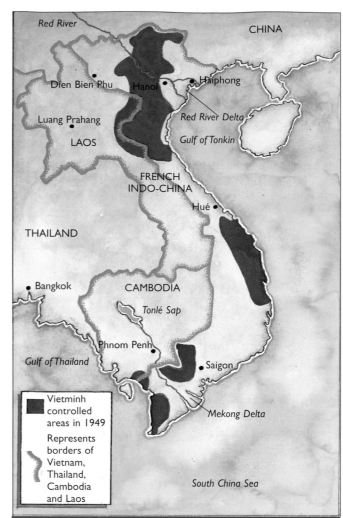

A The Vietminh in 1949 controlled a limited area of Vietnam. The most important areas were the ones where the most people lived. These were cities like Hanoi and Saigon and the Red River and Mekong deltas.

spread of communism. Ho Chi Minh was a communist and so the Americans would do whatever they could to help the French defeat him. In July 1950 – a month after the **Korean War** broke out – President Truman agreed to send the French $15 million of supplies. In fact, the United States was to spend nearly $3 billion in the next four years helping the French.

Communist victory in the East

The victory of Mao Zedong's communist forces in the war in China in 1949 was a great boost to the Vietminh. Mao provided his fellow communists in the jungles of north Vietnam with essential military supplies, such as artillery. Mao's victory was another reason why the Americans' attitude to the French changed. Communism seemed about to sweep its way across South East Asia and it had to be stopped. Vietnam would be a good place to do it – especially if the French were doing the fighting.

> **B** Not all opinion in the American government thought it was a good idea to oppose Ho Chi Minh. One official in the State Department, which dealt with foreign affairs, wrote a report in 1950. In it he warned:
>
> **Whether the French like it or not, independence is coming to Indo-China. Why, therefore, do we tie ourselves to the tail of their battered kite?**

'Elephant fights Grasshopper'

Ho Chi Minh liked to compare the Vietminh forces to a grasshopper fighting the French elephant. The reality was rather different because the Vietminh forces were not at all like feeble grasshoppers. By 1950 Giap commanded an army of over 100 000 men, well supplied with modern weapons and even trucks brought across the border from China. The French had 100 000 troops plus the support of 300 000 Vietnamese but these were not enough. The French were trying to control an area of 130 000 square kilometres of dense forest. It was an impossible task.

As long as the Vietminh played a waiting game, they could not be beaten. Safe in their jungle hideouts, they would strike out on hit-and-run attacks on French patrols and then retreat back into the forests. However, in 1950 and 1951 Giap made the mistake of moving from this guerrilla war style of fighting to big attacks on well-defended French positions. In one attack, 50 kilometres north of Hanoi, in January 1951 Giap lost 14 000 casualties, either killed or wounded, out of 20 000 Vietminh forces.

Dien Bien Phu

Giap was still determined to take on the French in a big, decisive battle. He chose a small village, Dien Bien Phu, close to the border with Laos. He knew the French would defend their position there as it would stop the Vietminh from getting into Laos for extra supplies of food. Patiently, Giap secretly assembled a vast army of 60 000 men with 200 heavy artillery guns on the high ground surrounding the French garrison of 15 000 troops.

This time, Giap did not launch a headlong attack against the French. Instead, he used his artillery to shell the French troops while his men dug tunnels to get them close to the enemy positions. This took two months. By the middle of March 1954 Giap was ready to attack. The French could not keep their troops properly supplied. On 7 May 1954 the surviving 10 000 French troops, half of them wounded, were forced to surrender. The rest were dead. Dien Bien Phu finally snapped the French will to fight on. They knew the war was lost.

C French prisoners after surrendering to the Vietminh at Dien Bien Phu.

1 Why was the United States sympathetic towards the Vietminh to begin with?
2 What do you think the writer of source B meant by the phrase: 'Why, therefore, do we tie ourselves to the tail of their battered kite?'?
3 The views of the writer of source B were ignored by the American government. Can you suggest any reasons for this? (Note the date it was written and think about other events in South East Asia.)
4 What does source A suggest about the strength of the Vietminh in the south? What reason can you give for this?
5 Here are five possible reasons why the Vietminh defeated the French. Look at each one and explain whether you think the reason is a good one or not and then list them in order of importance.
   a) The French had fewer troops than the Vietminh.
   b) The Vietminh used more appropriate tactics for where they were fighting.
   c) The French didn't get enough support from the United States.
   d) The Chinese provided vital supplies for the Vietminh.
   e) The Vietminh passionately believed in their cause.

American Involvement in the 1950s

Why did the United States get involved?
Why was Diem's government unpopular?

The Geneva Agreement

The French asked President Eisenhower of the United States to send American troops to help. There was even mention of using nuclear weapons. Eisenhower said 'no' to both. The United States had just ended the war in Korea in which over 40 000 Americans had died. They were in no mood to see more Americans die in Vietnam.

Britain, France, China, the Soviet Union, the United States, and Vietnam had already arranged to meet in May 1954 in Geneva, Switzerland. They met the day after Dien Bien Phu fell. Eisenhower wanted the French to carry on fighting but they had had enough. The Vietminh wanted early elections so the people could elect a government for the whole of Vietnam. They were confident of winning. The western powers (Britain, France and the United States) wanted a long delay before elections. They were worried by Ho Chi Minh's popularity throughout Vietnam.

Eventually, the following points were agreed:

- Vietnam would be divided temporarily in two along the 17th parallel – the North under Ho Chi Minh and the South under Ngo Dinh Diem.
- The Vietminh forces would withdraw from the South and the French would pull out of the North.
- A date for the elections was fixed: July 1956.

In eight years of fighting, 400 000 soldiers and civilians had died. But few at the time believed that the Geneva Agreement really would end the conflict. For one thing, the leader of the South, Ngo Dinh Diem, refused to accept the agreement. The Americans made it clear that they would support Diem because he was a strong enemy of communism.

The domino theory

Eisenhower's foreign policy followed what was called the '**domino theory**'. This was the idea that the countries of South East Asia (and elsewhere) were closely linked together. If one fell to communism, then others would also fall, like a row of dominoes. China became communist in 1949. North Korea and North Vietnam also had communist governments. If the South Vietnamese 'domino' followed, who would be next? Malaya? Burma?

Eisenhower was determined that communism would stop at the 17th parallel. Diem was 'elected' President of South Vietnam (officially called the Republic of Vietnam) in October 1955. The United States would therefore have to prop up Diem's government in the South with money, supplies and military equipment. Eisenhower knew that Diem's government would have to win the support of the people of South Vietnam. The fact that Diem was a Catholic while most Vietnamese were Buddhists wouldn't make this any easier.

'Re-education' Diem style

The statistics for Diem's election in 1955 tell a great deal about the kind of government Diem planned and the kind of man the United States was

Map labels:
CHINA
Red River
Hanoi
Dien Bien Phu
LAOS
NORTH VIETNAM
Vientiane
Gulf of Tonkin
THAILAND
Huế
Bangkok
CAMBODIA
Tonlé Sap
Phnom Penh
Saigon
SOUTH VIETNAM
Gulf of Thailand
South China Sea

Communist North Vietnam: led by Ho Chi Minh (1946–69); backed by the Soviet Union and China

17th parallel which divided Vietnam into North and South until elections planned for July 1956

South Vietnam: led by Ngo Dinh Diem (1955–63) who refused to hold elections in 1956; backed by the United States

● Major battle

A Vietnam after the Geneva Agreement, July 1954.

backing. Diem won with 98.2 per cent of the votes. The Americans had wisely advised him to claim only 60 or 70 per cent of the vote in his support. In Saigon there were 450 000 people entitled to vote. Somehow, 605 000 people voted for Diem! Clearly Diem had cheated in the elections.

Eisenhower hoped Diem would carry out land reforms to help the peasants of the South get land of their own. But Diem was not interested in land reform. The minister in charge of the land reform wasn't interested either. He was a big landowner. Land abandoned by its owners during the war was taken from the peasants who were now farming it. Those few peasants who did get land had to pay for it in instalments. However, when the Vietminh distributed land, they gave it to the peasants.

Diem was only interested in hunting down supporters of the Vietminh and 're-educating' them in prison camps. Those who couldn't be persuaded to change their views were executed. Perhaps as many as 12 000 were permanently 're-educated' in this way.

Diem: the puppet who pulled his own strings

The July date for the 1956 election for the whole of Vietnam came and went. There was no election. Diem refused to allow an election in the South. Eisenhower didn't try to make him have one either. Diem knew that the United States would have to go on supporting him because he prevented a communist victory in the South. As one American official put it, Diem was 'a puppet who pulled his own strings – and ours as well.'

Diem's government favoured the landowners at the expense of the peasants. The landowners forced their peasant tenants to pay high taxes and even made them work for nothing at certain times of the year. The communists in the South knew that the peasants wanted to fight back. Diem's attack on the Vietminh was proving very successful. Vietminh supporters in the South were gradually being eliminated by Diem's police and army. It was time to fight back.

The war begins again

Eventually, in 1959 the communist government in the North issued orders to the Vietminh to begin a terror campaign against officials of Diem's government. Between 1959 and 1961 on average 4000 South Vietnamese officials a year were assassinated by the 'Vietcong'. The term Vietcong means Vietnamese communist. The Americans decided that the government of South Vietnam should use this term rather than Vietminh. Vietminh stood for patriotism and it was bad propaganda for this idea to be linked to the communists in the North. The Americans thought that anything with 'communist' in it was an insult.

B A Vietnamese bus driver told an American journalist, Stanley Karnow, how one Vietcong assassination squad operated:

Five or six Vietcong guys stopped my bus one morning to check the identity cards of the passengers. They dragged two men off the bus and their chief said to them, 'We've been waiting for you. We've warned you many times to leave your jobs, but you haven't obeyed. So now we must carry out the sentence.'

They forced the two men to kneel by the roadside, and one of the Vietcong guys chopped off their heads with a machete. They pinned their verdicts to their shirts saying the murdered men were policemen …

Afterwards, the Vietcong guys gave the passengers back their identity cards, saying, 'You'll get into trouble with the authorities without these.'

Q

1 Why did the United States refuse to send troops to help the French against the Vietminh in 1954?
2 Why do you think the western powers at Geneva wanted to delay the elections in Vietnam?
3 What do you suppose the American official meant when he said that Diem was 'a puppet who pulled his own strings – and ours as well'?
4 Why do you think the two policemen in source B were executed by the Vietcong?
5 How useful do you think source B is in explaining the reasons for the popularity of the Vietcong among the ordinary Vietnamese people? Think about the source's **provenance** as well as what it says.
6 Why did the government of Diem fail to win the support of ordinary Vietnamese? What do you think was the most important reason? You should comment on the following points:
   a) Vietnamese patriotism
   b) foreign support for Diem
   c) land reform
   d) religion.

American Support for South Vietnam, 1961–64

How did American involvement increase? Why was Diem unable to defeat the NLF?

In December 1960 the communists in Hanoi set up the National Liberation Front in the South. The NLF, though, did not consist only of communists. It had broad appeal to middle-class professionals such as doctors and teachers, as well as peasants and workers. Its main aims were to overthrow Diem, get rid of the Americans, and reunite North and South Vietnam. A month after the NLF was created, John F. Kennedy became president of the United States.

'Crazier than hell'?

Kennedy wanted the American people to think he was tough on communism. He was keen to increase American involvement in South Vietnam but he would not send United States combat troops there. He agreed to increase the number of military experts training the South Vietnamese Army, the Army of the Republic of Vietnam (ARVN). These went up from 700 to 3000. By 1963 there were 16 000 of them. He also agreed to equip a further 20 000 troops for the ARVN. This brought the size of the South Vietnamese Army to 170 000 men. They were all paid for by the US.

The issue of combat troops continued to come up. One of Kennedy's advisers suggested that one day there would be 300 000 American combat troops in Vietnam. Kennedy laughed, 'Well, George, you're supposed to be one of the smartest guys in town, but you're crazier than hell. That will never happen.' In 1968 the number of American soldiers in Vietnam stood at 536 000.

A United States troop levels in Vietnam 1965–72.

In 1961 the United States spent nearly $270 million in military support for Diem. The ARVN numbered 170 000 troops but the number of Vietcong was estimated at just 10 000. The question the Americans should have asked themselves was this: why did it take an army of 170 000 to defeat one of just 10 000? The real point was that there wasn't a *military* solution to the Vietcong (VC). The only chance that Diem and the Americans had to defeat the VC was to undermine the popularity of the communists in the South. To do this they had to show that they could help the people as much, if not more.

> Vice President Johnson in 1961: 'President Diem is the Churchill of the decade.'

The 'strategic hamlet' policy

Diem's solution in 1962 to NLF popularity in the South was to take the peasants away from areas where the NLF was strong. Sympathetic villages were providing food and passing intelligence information about ARVN activities in the area to the VC. Diem's 'strategic hamlet' programme was supposed to stop the villagers helping the communists in the South. It meant moving entire villages many kilometres away from their homes. The population was re-housed in a new location, 'protected' from the Vietcong by South Vietnamese troops.

The peasants were then told they had to pay the South Vietnamese government officials for the building materials to rebuild their homes. They even had to pay for the barbed wire to protect them from the VC. These items, of course, had been provided by the United States for *free* distribution to the Vietnamese families involved.

By the summer of 1963 over two-thirds of the population had been moved to these strategic hamlets. This system had been used successfully against communists by the British in Malaya in the 1950s. The big difference was that food was hard to come by in Malaya. In Vietnam it was easy to get hold of. The NLF did not starve. Neither were they cut off from the peasants. In many cases the NLF already had supporters inside the villages.

All that happened was that Diem had now moved communist supporters to a new area in which they could spread their ideas. Those villagers who weren't already in the NLF often became supporters because of the way they were treated. The strategic hamlet programme was a terrible flop.

In January 1963 a fight took place near the village of Ap Bac, about 60 kilometres from Saigon. About 350 Vietcong guerrillas were forced into a battle by over 2000 South Vietnamese troops, backed up by United States helicopters with their American crews. The prospects for a stunning victory looked good. Instead, five of the helicopters were shot down and three American crewmen killed. Sixty South Vietnamese troops also died. Just three VC bodies were found.

B The Americans thought they could win over the 'hearts and minds' of the South Vietnamese by showing them the benefits of the American way of life. Somewhere down the list, after napalm and cluster bombs, came baseball.

The American adviser to the ARVN forces in the area, Lieutenant Colonel Vann, was angered by the failure of the ARVN commanders to work together. They squabbled with each other and at one point confused South Vietnamese troops ended up firing at each other. Vann quit his job. He argued that the war was being fought very badly by the South Vietnamese. The United States government was covering up the fact so as not to spoil relations with Diem.

'Traitors, crackpots or madmen'?

The press in the United States was also being kept in the dark about the war at this time. Kennedy denied that there were any American troops involved in combat in Vietnam. But American jet pilots were bombing and machine-gunning NLF areas. Helicopter pilots were also transporting

ARVN forces into combat zones. After the battle at Ap Bac an American journalist asked an American military spokesman a tough question about the battle. The spokesman snapped back, 'Get on team.'

American officials in the United States Information Service (USIS) were aware that they were losing the **propaganda** war to the NLF. In 1962 USIS came up with the idea of a competition for a new name for the enemy. Vietcong wasn't suitable any longer. 'Viet' was wrong because it implied that the enemy was still patriotic and 'Cong' (communist) was also wrong because most peasants wouldn't know what that meant anyway. The head of USIS wanted a term which would show the Vietcong as 'traitors … crackpots or madmen'. It's not clear which entry (if there were any) won the top prize of $47. Perhaps the competition says more about the USIS than its enemy.

C A recent book outlines the details of the USIS competition in 1962.

The new head of USIS wanted a term for the enemy which would … 'influence the Vietnamese people to regard the enemy in the most important (in your view) of the following ways … as arrogant bullies, as foreign and/or Chinese puppets, as common criminals, with hatred, as traitors, as hypocrites, as crackpots or madmen, as children playing soldier, or as bloodthirsty murderers. Perhaps … a term about the way they lecture everyone for hours and make the villagers under their control learn silly songs and slogans?'

1 What were the aims of the NLF?
2 Why was the 'strategic hamlet' policy such a failure?
3 What does the battle of Ap Bac suggest about the military abilities of the South Vietnamese? Explain your answer.
4 a) What do you suppose the spokesman meant by the phrase 'Get on team'?
   b) What does it suggest about the United States military's attitude to the role of the American media in the war?
5 'The biggest mistake the Americans made in the early stages of the war was that they underestimated the people they were fighting.' Using the sources in the book so far and your own knowledge, explain whether you agree or disagree with this interpretation.

Why did the Americans support the over-throw of Diem?

Death by burning

On 11 June 1963 a 66-year-old Buddhist monk sat down in the middle of a busy Saigon road. He crossed his legs and held his palms together in an act of prayer. Other Buddhist monks crowded round and one of them poured a can of petrol over his orange robe. The monk calmly lit a match and set himself alight. The man remained sitting for ten minutes as the flames covered his body. Eventually he toppled over. An American photographer, tipped off in advance, was there to take a photograph which stunned the world. Why had this monk burned himself to death?

A This Buddhist monk was only the first of several who burned themselves to death in protest against Diem's government. Diem's harsh reaction to the Buddhists convinced the United States government that Diem had to go.

Diem, a strong Catholic, had promoted many fellow Catholics to important jobs in the government and the army. Vietnam's Buddhists, who made up most of the population, resented this favouritism. But the real cause of their anger was Diem's anti-Buddhist policies. Buddhists, unlike Catholics, had to have government permission to carry out their acts of worship.

Buddhist opposition

Diem also had a law which banned all flags except the flag of Vietnam. When Catholics in Hué flew the flag of the Catholic Church the police took no action. In May 1963 the Buddhists decided to test the law by flying the Buddhist flag during celebrations of the Buddha's birthday. Troops opened fire on the celebrating crowd. Nine people were killed, eight of them children. Two days later, on 10 May, 10 000 Buddhists marched in protest. Diem ordered the arrest of leading Buddhists and their supporters.

These actions led to the suicide by burning of the Buddhist monk. The protests and the suicide got a great deal of publicity in the United States. For the first time the American media were covering stories about Diem's government and its unpopularity rather than about the war. The South Vietnamese government claimed the monks were working for the communists and disregarded official American protests. Diem's sister-in-law, Madame Nhu, did not help matters when she told American officials, 'If the Buddhists wish to have another barbecue, I will be glad to supply the petrol and a match.'

The *coup d'état*

President Kennedy realised that Diem was too unpopular to defeat Vietcong. The government in Washington gave its approval to a plot or *coup d'état* to overthrow Diem and his brother, Nhu, who was Diem's chief adviser. There were government advisers in Washington who were worried about the coup. What if the anti-Diem plotters weren't strong enough to get rid of Diem straight away and there was a civil war? What if the generals who replaced Diem were no better or started fighting among themselves?

Nhu wasn't stupid. He realised that some generals were planning a coup against him and he had a plan of his own to deal with them. Unfortunately for Nhu, the general he revealed this plan to was also one of the plotters. They decided, therefore, to attack before Nhu and Diem could put *their* plan into operation.

The troops supporting the coup surrounded Diem's palace in Saigon on 1 November 1963. They didn't attack it. At this stage the plan was simply to force Diem and his brother to leave the country and not to kill them. The brothers managed to escape from the palace. Diem appealed to the American ambassador, Cabot Lodge, for help but none was offered. The next day they agreed to surrender on the condition that they would be allowed to leave the country. They gave themselves up.

They agreed to be taken in an armoured car for their 'protection'. A few moments later they were both shot dead. The people of Saigon cheered when they heard the news but Kennedy was stunned. The killing of Diem and his brother was not part of the plan. Three weeks later, Kennedy would also be dead. The general who took Diem's place lasted three months.

B When Madame Nhu wasn't offering to help 'barbecue' Buddhist monks, she could be seen instructing her own women's section of the South Vietnamese Army. Madame Nhu, the sister-in-law of Diem, meddled in political affairs and managed to increase Diem's unpopularity. This wasn't easy to do because his government was already remarkably unpopular.

The bully at the porch

The new military rulers of South Vietnam tried to improve relations with all the groups Diem had treated badly or ignored, such as Buddhists, students and professional people. Buddhists were freed from prison. The government stated that its aim was a neutral South Vietnam in which the NLF would be allowed to exist. Foreign troops, eventually, would leave. This was not what the Americans wanted to hear. The new president, Lyndon Johnson, wanted to show that he was tough on communism as well.

The United States wanted a more aggressive war against the communists in Hanoi, not a 'softly softly' approach. Johnson's version of the domino theory was typically direct: 'If you let a bully come into your front yard [garden] one day, the next day he'll be up on your porch, and the day after that he'll rape your wife in your own bed.'

The United States didn't think the new government was capable of keeping the North Vietnamese 'bully' out of the neighbourhood, let alone the porch. The Americans, therefore, supported yet another coup in January 1964. The new military ruler, General Khanh, promised a more effective war against the communists. Khanh lasted a year.

A more effective war was certainly needed and urgently. In 1957 the Vietminh had numbered just 2000. By the beginning of 1963 the number of Vietminh (or Vietcong) fighters had increased to only 23 000. But Diem's unpopular and corrupt government had encouraged a rapid growth in Vietcong support. By January 1965 there were 170 000 VC fighters operating in the South. Most of these new recruits came from the South but some were North Vietnamese Army (NVA) – trained soldiers from the North.

> An official of Diem's government said: 'Apart from the colour of our skin, we are no different from the French.'

1 Why did the Buddhist monk burn himself to death?
2 Why did the Americans decide to support the overthrow of Diem?
3 The photographer who took the photograph (source A) had been tipped off in advance by the Buddhist opposition to Diem.
   a) What does this suggest about the incident?
   b) Does this make the source more or less useful to a historian?
4 What point do you think Johnson was making in the quotation about the bully?
5 'The Americans were no longer just advisers in South Vietnam. They were really running the country.' What evidence can you find from what you have read so far to support this interpretation?

The Gulf of Tonkin

Why did the United States send combat troops to Vietnam?

The Americans had hoped that they might be able to pay for and train an effective South Vietnamese Army to fight the Vietcong. In this way the United States could avoid using their own troops. Paying for the army wasn't a problem. The American advisers did their best to train it. But they couldn't give it the *will* to fight.

The Vietcong, on the other hand, had tremendous morale. In fact, the Vietcong no longer depended on weapons from the North because they had captured as many as 200 000 American guns from the South Vietnamese by the middle of 1964. The North didn't need to send them.

A Two Vietcong guerrillas prepare a trap for use against American troops. It was set into action by a trip wire. The trap, hidden high up, swung down from its position and the spikes impaled the victim.

In early 1964 the United States military prepared plans for the bombing of North Vietnam. The air force commander recommended bombing North Vietnam because 'we are swatting flies when we should be going after the manure pile'. But they needed information on the anti-aircraft systems the communist government in the North had set up around their main cities and along the coast. Secret South Vietnamese commando raids were planned to find this out.

The Gulf of Tonkin incident

South Vietnamese commandos attacked North Vietnamese radar stations in the Gulf of Tonkin during the night of 31 July 1964. The American destroyer, *USS Maddox*, assisted in the attack by monitoring the signals sent out by the radar stations. This would help to locate their positions. On the morning of 2 August three North Vietnamese torpedo boats headed straight for the *Maddox*, which was still in the area.

> Only two senators voted against the Gulf of Tonkin resolution. 82 supported it.

The *Maddox* opened fire and the torpedo boats each fired a torpedo at the American ship. Two of the torpedoes missed and the third hit the ship but didn't explode. United States jets sank one of the boats and damaged the other two. Johnson decided to play down this incident as there were no American casualties. But he ordered the *Maddox* to stay in the area.

The flying fish that fired 'torpedoes'

During the night of 3 August the captain of the *Maddox* reported that his ship and the *USS Joy* were being attacked by torpedoes. For four hours the two ships blasted away at an enemy they never saw. Not one sailor actually saw or heard communist gunfire. United States jet pilots over the 'battle' zone reported that they saw no evidence of the enemy. Johnson, this time, decided that the United States would strike back. The jet pilots changed their first reports to support the 'evidence' that there had been an attack.

There was a presidential election due in November and Johnson's Republican opponent had claimed that Johnson was 'soft' on communism. This incident gave the President the chance to prove the opposite. United States jets were ordered to attack North Vietnamese torpedo boat bases and about 25 of these were destroyed. Johnson knew that there had been no second attack. Two or three days later he told an official, 'Hell, those dumb, stupid sailors were just shooting at flying fish.'

Congress believed that a second attack had taken place and that the North needed to be taught a lesson. Johnson proposed 'the Gulf of Tonkin' resolution to Congress on 7 August. The resolution or law gave the President the power to take any military measures he thought necessary to defend 'freedom' in South East Asia, including South Vietnam. Johnson now had the power to escalate or step up the level of American military involvement. But he wasn't yet willing to do this. Johnson and his advisers believed that further air attacks, if needed, would be enough to bring victory.

But it soon became clear that the Vietcong would prove impossible to beat by using only the South Vietnamese Army. In just two battles in December 1964 two battalions of elite, specially trained South Vietnamese troops were effectively destroyed in Vietcong ambushes. Over 700 were killed, wounded or captured – and these were the best the ARVN had to offer. What chance did the rest of the South Vietnamese Army stand? United States air bases were also attacked by the NLF. In February 1965 the NLF guerrillas destroyed ten American helicopters, killed eight servicemen, and wounded over 100.

B A United States adviser shows a group of South Vietnamese soldiers how to use a bayonet. A frightening weapon perhaps, but the bayonet in Vietnam proved more useful for opening cans of fruit.

Two fateful steps

A week later, on 13 February, the President gave his approval to 'Operation Rolling Thunder'. This meant the bombing of North Vietnam on a regular basis. It was a major escalation of the

United States' role in the war and it was quickly followed by another. In March 3500 United States combat troops arrived in Vietnam to protect the air bases being used to bomb North Vietnam. By the end of the year there would be 200 000 of them. America's war had begun.

C Johnson's message to Congress, 5 August 1964 (adapted):

... The threat to the free nations of South East Asia has long been clear. The North Vietnamese regime has constantly tried to take over South Vietnam and Laos. This communist regime has broken the Geneva Agreement for Vietnam. It has continually organised a secret and illegal campaign against the government, which includes the direction, training and supply of personnel and arms for the conduct of guerrilla warfare in South Vietnamese territory ...

As President of the United States I have decided that I should now ask the Congress to join in making clear the national determination that all such attacks will be opposed, and that the United States will continue in its basic policy of assisting the free nations of the area to defend their freedom.

---

1 What was the major difference between the troops of South Vietnam and the Vietcong?
2 How did America's role in Vietnam suddenly escalate in early 1965?
3 What do you think the air force commander meant by 'we are swatting flies when we should be going after the manure pile'?
4 There never was a second Gulf of Tonkin incident. Why do you think Johnson acted as though there had been a second communist attack?
5 What incidents in late 1964 and early 1965 helped to convince the Americans that they would have to send in their own troops?
6 In his speech to Congress in August 1964 Johnson claimed that:
   a) North Vietnam had broken the Geneva Agreement of 1954;
   b) North Vietnam was supplying weapons and troops to the Vietcong in the South;
   c) the United States was helping 'free nations' like South Vietnam defend their freedom from communism.
   Comment on each of these claims, saying whether you think they are true or not.

Tactics and Attitudes

What tactics did each side use? How successful were they? What were the attitudes on each side?

'Operation Rolling Thunder' – the American bombing campaign over North Vietnam – was supposed to last eight weeks. It lasted three and a half years. During the war, the United States Air Force dropped more bombs on North Vietnam than *all* the bombs dropped in the Second World War. But the bombing of cities by both sides did not have a decisive impact on that war.

Some United States advisers told Johnson that Rolling Thunder would not achieve any significant results in this war either. North Vietnam had few factories to bomb. It was mostly countryside and the bombing would have little effect. The supporters of bombing claimed that the campaign would destroy North Vietnam's supply routes to the NLF in the South. In this way, the Vietcong would soon run out of weapons and equipment. Johnson also believed that bombing would convince the North that the United States wouldn't give up and this would persuade the North to agree to a compromise.

A American troops carrying out a 'search and destroy' mission. This soldier is using his Zippo lighter to set fire to a Vietnamese peasant's home.

Defensive strategy

It was essential to defend the air bases from which the bombers flew. The United States troops which arrived in South Vietnam were under orders to defend only these air bases. They also protected the ports where supplies and more troops arrived.

These troops were allowed to patrol up to a maximum of 80 kilometres around the bases to make sure that there were no VC in the area.

Johnson hoped that adopting a basically defensive strategy would make it more acceptable to American public opinion. A few months later Johnson told General Westmoreland, the commander of the American forces in Vietnam, that his troops could follow more aggressive tactics. The American public wasn't told this.

Search and destroy

Westmoreland's basic strategy was that the American troops would search out and destroy the big enemy forces and the regular or professional troops of the North Vietnamese Army (NVA) operating in the South. This would leave the South Vietnamese troops to deal with the less well-trained guerrilla forces or Vietcong. Westmoreland was convinced that his troops would defeat their enemy because they were better equipped and had the benefit of artillery and air support.

Searching out and destroying the enemy was one thing. But all too often the enemy could not be found, let alone destroyed. Frustrated and frightened American troops settled on searching out villages and destroying those instead. In most cases, these villages played no role in supporting the VC. The troops came to call these operations 'Zippo' raids after the name of the lighters they used to set fire to the thatched houses of the Vietnamese villagers.

The pattern of the war was quickly set. United States forces, when they came across the Vietcong, would often inflict heavy casualties on them. Air strikes proved particularly effective. In November 1965, for example, the Americans fought their first battle against NVA forces in the Ia Drang Valley. The NVA lost an estimated 1800 men killed as against 240 American troops dead in the four day battle. But the North Vietnamese retreated into neutral Cambodia and the United States forces couldn't follow. Later, the NVA force would reappear in South Vietnam, after making up its losses.

General Westmoreland was pleased with the result. The 'kill ratio' was favourable: one American killed for nearly every eight communists. Over 33 000 American artillery shells and 7000 rockets had been fired in the battle. All this helped to convince him that the 'search and destroy' strategy was right and that superior United States fire-power would always guarantee victory in this kind of confrontation. The North Vietnamese, he believed, couldn't survive casualties like these for long. But he was wrong.

Of the 58 000 American soldiers killed in Vietnam, 3104 were 18 years old or younger.

The NVA – learning lessons

This was the big difference between the sides. The communists were so committed to their cause that they would accept these losses. Westmoreland thought that American public opinion would do the same. But he was, once again, wrong.

The North Vietnamese also learned an important tactical lesson from the battle. In future, the regular NVA troops and Vietcong would try to avoid pitched battles with the enemy. Hit-and-run guerrilla raids and ambushes would mean fewer casualties. If they had to fight the Americans in big battles, then they would try to keep as close as they could to them during the fighting. This would make it difficult for the American troops to call in artillery fire or air strikes since these might hit their own forces as well.

The Australians

B The Vietcong feared Australian troops more than American ones.

Australia agreed to send troops to Vietnam. The Australians also had reason to worry about the domino theory. They feared the spread of communism in South East Asia and by 1969 there were about 7000 Australian troops in Vietnam. One Vietcong fighter considered the Australians to be better jungle fighters with better tactics than the United States troops, as source C tells us.

C Trinh Duc was a communist from 1942 until the late 1970s. However, he was of Chinese origin. In the late 1970s the communist government of a reunified Vietnam harshly treated Vietnamese of Chinese origin. So he fled from Vietnam and settled in the United States where he told his story of the war against the United States in the 1960s:

There was no way we could stand up to the Americans. Every time they came in force we ran from them. Then when they turned back, we'd follow them. We practically lived on top of them, so they couldn't hit us with artillery and air strikes …

Worse than the Americans were the Australians. The Americans' style was to hit us, then call for planes and artillery. Our response was to break contact and disappear if we could, but if we couldn't we'd move up right next to them so the planes couldn't get at us. The Australians were more patient than the Americans, better guerrilla fighters, better at ambushes. They liked to stay with us instead of calling in the planes. We were more afraid of their style.

1 Why did some United States advisers think that the bombing of Vietnam would not achieve important results?

2 What evidence is there in the text that Johnson was worried about the reaction of the American public to growing involvement in the war?

3 Why were the Americans always likely to win pitched battles against the VC or North Vietnamese Army (NVA)?

4 According to source C, what were the main differences between the American and Australian styles of fighting?

5 a) Is there anything in the provenance of source C which might make you doubt its reliability?

b) Is there anything in the content (what the source says) which might make you doubt its reliability?

c) Do you think Trinh Duc, therefore, is a reliable source? Explain your reasons, after thinking about your answers to (a) and (b).

What were attitudes on each side?

Americans tended to accept that the NVA were very good soldiers. They wore uniforms and fought the Americans and South Vietnamese on equal terms. But attitudes to the Vietcong were very different. They were not regular troops. They were guerrilla fighters. They wore the traditional, civilian black 'pyjamas' of the Vietnamese peasant and couldn't be recognised as guerrillas. The United States forces found this kind of warfare very frustrating. All the same, American troops could respect astonishing courage wherever it came from, as source A tells us.

A This wounded VC guerrilla is being looked after by United States troops. Terribly wounded in the stomach, he had carried his intestines around with him for three days in a bowl. When he asked for a drink, the South Vietnamese interpreter refused. An angry American soldier offered the Vietcong his canteen instead, saying, 'Any soldier who can fight three days with his insides out can drink from my canteen anytime.'

Body count

Westmoreland was convinced that the war would be won by killing large numbers of the enemy. This was a similar attitude to that of the First World War generals. The chief aim of the United States infantry was to get a high enemy 'body count'. The problem was that the NVA and VC were prepared to suffer high casualties and the Americans always exaggerated the number of the enemy they killed anyway.

B One American reporter told of an incident involving a US Special Forces captain who told him:

I went out and killed one VC and freed a prisoner. Next day the major called me in and told me that I'd killed fourteen VC and freed six prisoners. You want to see the medal?

The best way to get a high body count was to send out a patrol as bait. If the NVA or VC had more men than the patrol they might attack it. The attacked patrol would then call in the air strikes or artillery fire. These tactics could cause terrible casualties but it was never easy for the Americans to be sure of the numbers.

The communist troops tried very hard to take their dead and wounded with them. This meant that often the body count would be disappointingly low. Neither side bothered with enemy wounded. It was too difficult to care for them and get them back for treatment. They were generally shot. Healthy prisoners had a better chance of being taken back for interrogation – and probably torture.

C Occasionally some compassion could be shown for the enemy – in this case a female NVA nurse shot by an American soldier. The incident is taken from a book written by a sergeant in the United States army who served in Vietnam.

She had been shot once. The bullet tore through her green uniform and into her buttock and went out through her groin. She moaned a little, not much, but she screamed when the medic touched at her wound. Like a pair of twin fountains, blood gushed out of the holes, front and back.

Her face lay on some dirt. Flies were all over her, feeding on her blood ... There was no shade. It was mid-afternoon of a hot day.

'She's a pretty woman, pretty for a gook [Vietnamese]. You don't see many pretty gooks, that's damn sure.'

'Look at that blood come, Jesus. Like a waterfall, like Niagara Falls. She's gonna die quick. Can't mend up them bullet holes, no way. She's wasted.'

'I wish I could help her.' The man who shot her knelt down. 'Can't carry her, she won't let us. She's NVA, green uniform and everything. Hell, she's probably an NVA nurse, she probably knows she's just going to die. Look at her squeeze her hands and rock. She's just trying to hurry and press all the blood out of herself.'

Defoliants

If the enemy couldn't be forced into battle, then the villages in the surrounding area became the target instead. Chemicals were sprayed in jungle areas to kill off the vegetation so that the Vietcong couldn't use the jungle for cover. But the United States also used these defoliants to destroy crops. This stopped the guerrillas getting food supplies and it also punished those villages suspected of helping the communists. On other occasions the villages were set alight.

All this was supposed to convince the peasants not to help the VC. With their crops destroyed, villagers had no choice but to re-settle in new villages away from VC controlled areas. This, of course, made it easier for the Americans and ARVN to isolate the guerrillas.

D Doug Ramsey was an American civilian who worked for the Agency for International Development (AID) in Vietnam. Its purpose was to bring supplies to South Vietnamese refugees. He was taken prisoner by the Vietcong in 1966. His captors took him to a village that had just been burned to the ground by some South Vietnamese troops. The author, Neil Sheehan, was a journalist in Vietnam, and told his story:

> The rubble of the hamlet was still smoking, and it was obvious that these people had returned only a short time before to discover what had happened to their homes. Children were whimpering ... Women were poking through the smouldering debris of the houses trying to save cooking utensils and any other small possessions that might have escaped the flames ...The soldiers had also burned all of the rice that had not been buried or hidden elsewhere and had shot the buffalo and other livestock and thrown the carcasses down the wells to poison the water supply.
>
> A middle-aged farmer in the group asked Ramsey what agency he worked for. 'AID' Ramsey said. 'AID!' the farmer cried. 'Look about you,' he said to Ramsey. He pointed, sweeping his finger from one charred ruin to another. 'Here is your American AID!' The farmer spat on the ground and walked away.

E A dead NVA soldier, his personal possessions scattered about him. Soldiers on both sides looted the dead for anything of value and sometimes mutilated their bodies. Ears were sometimes cut off by troops as 'trophies'.

1 What does source B suggest about how accurate United States estimates were of the numbers of enemy killed in action?
2 How do you think the incident in source D would have affected relations between South Vietnamese peasants and the American and South Vietnamese forces?
3 a) Study source C on page 15 and sources A, B, C and D on pages 16 and 17. What does each source suggest about why the Americans eventually lost the war?
   b) Which source do you think is most useful for this purpose? You should think about the provenance of the sources when explaining your answer.

The most used defoliant was Agent Orange. It was later discovered that Agent Orange contained a dioxin which caused cancer among those who used it or were affected by it. It also led to pregnant women giving birth to terribly deformed children. Traces of the chemical got washed by the rain into streams from which soldiers on both sides drank.

North Vietnam at War

How much support was there in the North for the war?

In 1959 the government of North Vietnam decided that the two halves of Vietnam, North and South, would never be reunited by peaceful means. From then on, Hanoi, the capital of North Vietnam, was committed to a campaign of guerrilla war to defeat the government of South Vietnam in Saigon. To begin with, Hanoi used local Vietminh or Vietcong forces in the South to organise guerrilla attacks and assassinations of prominent South Vietnamese officials.

Ho Chi Minh Trail

These local forces were kept supplied along the Ho Chi Minh Trail. By the end of the war, the Trail consisted of a network of 15 000 kilometres of roads through jungles and mountains. It ran from the north to the south through neutral Laos and Cambodia. There could be as many as ten different routes between two points. If one was bombed, then another could be used. Despite repeated bombing by the United States Air Force in attacks like Operation Rolling Thunder, it is likely that Hanoi managed to get at least two-thirds of its supplies through to the South.

A Some American advisers doubted that bombing could really reduce supplies to the South. Sophisticated roads weren't needed to shift supplies from the North by bicycle, as you can see in this photograph.

The NVA and Vietcong forces in the South in the early years of the war needed very little in the way of supplies. This made it much easier to keep them equipped. They had no aircraft, no tanks, no artillery, no weapons which a man couldn't carry. It has been estimated that they needed only 15 tons of supplies a day. Russia and China provided North Vietnam with 6000 tons a day. So only a tiny fraction of these supplies had to trickle down to the South to keep the war going.

'Born in the North to die in the South'

From 1960 onwards, Hanoi began sending regular troops from the North Vietnamese Army to the South. Many of these were volunteers but not all. The government of North Vietnam used **conscription** to maintain the size of its army. This became even more necessary after United States troops joined the war in 1965. From then on Hanoi sent 100 000 troops to the South each year. At least 500 000 and perhaps as many 900 000 of these died during the war. For a country of just 18 million, these were huge losses.

Many in North Vietnam welcomed the chance to fight for the liberation of South Vietnam from the '**puppet**' government of Diem and the generals who replaced him. Vietnamese nationalism, the desire to unite North and South and get rid of foreign control, was the most important reason for supporting Hanoi's campaign. Communism came second as a reason in the North for supporting the war.

Histories of the Vietnam War have tended to see the North as a country where *everybody* was *fully* committed to war. But not all North Vietnamese were enthusiastic about the war. There was a traditional hostility between the North and South and not all northerners thought that the South was worth dying for. Many dreaded their call-up notice telling them to join the NVA.

There was also, according to source B, resentment about the fact that often leading

NVA soldier: 'There was no way we could stand up to the Americans. Every time they came in force we ran from them. Then when they turned back, we'd follow them.'

members of the Communist Party in the North could arrange for their sons to avoid the call-up. This could be done by sending them abroad to other communist countries to study.

People were also made angry by the refusal of the government to tell families about casualties. The government was afraid that it would have a terrible effect on morale because so many NVA were being killed or wounded. Few of those sent south expected to return (see source B). For the same reason, badly wounded soldiers were kept from the public in remote highland areas in the North.

> **B** Le Thanh was a communist who lived in the North during the war. After the war he escaped to Hong Kong and then the United States. He told his story about his experiences in the North:

> I also asked questions about why nobody was coming back from the South. It began to seem like an open pit. The more young people who were lost there, the more they sent. There was even a kind of motto that the whole generation of army-age North Vietnamese adopted. They tattooed it on themselves and they sang songs about it – 'Born in the North to die in the South'.
>
> When soldiers died, most often word would get back to their families through friends who had returned because they had been wounded. Usually there was no official notification. Sometimes families would go to the government to ask for information. But it was a terrible situation for them, because anyone who spread word about soldiers dying would get into trouble with the police.

However, it is clear that North Vietnam would never have been able to fight the French and then the Americans – and beat them – without tremendous support from its people. The North was well organised to meet American bombing raids. The Soviet Union (communist Russia) provided 8000 anti-aircraft guns and 200 anti-aircraft missile sites. Air raid shelters, including individual ones sunk into pavements, provided further protection (see source C).

Despite this, somewhere in the region of 100 000 civilians were killed in air raids between 1965 and 1972. But the evidence suggests that the bombing only increased the determination of the people to carry on the war. The Americans were also hit hard by the bombing. 600 pilots were captured during the war and over 700 planes shot down by the end of 1967. Neither was the bombing 'cost effective'. It cost the United States ten dollars to cause one dollar's worth of damage to the North.

C Personal shelters like this in the North's major cities provided some protection against American bombs.

1 Why was the Ho Chi Minh Trail so important?
2 Why did the war remain popular in the North, despite the casualties?
3 What impression of the war in the North does source B give?
4 Look at the provenance of source B. Do you think this makes the source more or less reliable? Explain your answer.

Extended writing
'By the end of 1967 it was clear that the United States was losing the war in Vietnam.' Write an essay of about 300 words to explain whether you agree or disagree with this interpretation. The following issues may help you with your answer:
● the effectiveness of American bombing of the North;
● the effectiveness of the tactics used by the United States and the Vietcong;
● the attitude of the peasants of South Vietnam to each side;
● the commitment to the war shown by the troops of the United States, South Vietnam, the Vietcong, and North Vietnam.

The Tet Offensive, 1968

Who won the Tet Offensive?

On 31 January 1968 70 000 Vietcong launched a massive attack on 100 towns and cities in South Vietnam. It was launched during the Vietnamese New Year or Tet holiday. The Americans and South Vietnamese were taken by surprise because half the ARVN (South Vietnamese Army) was on leave for the Tet holiday. For the first time, the war came right into the cities. It was a war neither side was used to fighting. The Vietcong abandoned the guerrilla war style of fighting. Instead, they took on the United States and ARVN forces in a series of conventional battles.

> **American senator, 1968:** 'We are there not just to save the South Vietnamese. If we lose there, before you know it, they would be up to the beaches in Hawaii.'

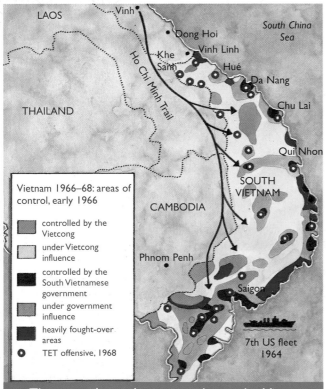

A The map shows how spread out the Vietcong attacks were in 1968. It also shows that most of the large, populated towns and cities were still in South Vietnamese hands.

Map labels: LAOS, Vinh, Dong Hoi, Vinh Linh, South China Sea, Khe Sanh, Hué, Ho Chi Minh Trail, Da Nang, THAILAND, Chu Lai, Qui Nhon, SOUTH VIETNAM, CAMBODIA, Phnom Penh, Saigon, 7th US fleet 1964

Vietnam 1966–68: areas of control, early 1966
- controlled by the Vietcong
- under Vietcong influence
- controlled by the South Vietnamese government
- under government influence
- heavily fought-over areas
- ⊙ TET offensive, 1968

This city war was also one the VC were not equipped to fight. They found themselves forced to hold positions which they couldn't really defend. In the jungle they would simply have melted away. There they always avoided fighting battles where the odds were against them. In the Tet Offensive they couldn't do this and paid the penalty.

Why did the VC launch the Tet Offensive?

By the end of 1967 the war was bogged down in a stalemate. The communist forces couldn't match the Americans' firepower. They couldn't beat them in normal battles without the aircraft, tanks and helicopters the United States had. On the other hand, the American forces didn't have enough men to pursue the VC deep into their jungle hideouts. They were stretched to the maximum just defending their own camps and bases.

The government in Hanoi knew that public opinion in the United States would not allow more troops to be sent to Vietnam. Therefore, the North believed the Americans could never win the war. Hanoi hoped that the Tet Offensive would make the Americans realise this more quickly.

The communist government in Hanoi had important political objectives for the offensive. They hoped that the local South Vietnamese population would rise up in support and help them overthrow the Saigon government. They also hoped that the United States would realise that they couldn't win the war and so begin to withdraw their forces. If nothing else happened, this at least would leave the South Vietnamese on their own.

Saigon shock

There's no doubting the dramatic impact the attacks had on United States and world opinion. One of the most remarkable events was the attack by a 15-man suicide squad of VC guerrillas who fought their way into the American embassy in Saigon. They held out for six hours before being killed. American television showed film of the attack to 50 million homes in the United States. The American public was astonished by what they saw. The embassy was the symbol of the American presence in Vietnam and it wasn't safe from the enemy. If the embassy couldn't be defended, then what could?

Horror in Hué

The National Liberation Front (NLF) also attacked Hué, a major city further north. They held it for 25 days until ARVN and United States forces recaptured the city. Before this could take place, though, the VC executed about 3000 civilians. Their 'crime' was that they had links with the South Vietnamese government as officials or army officers. Basically, they killed anyone they considered hostile to the NLF. Some historians say 3000 deaths is an exaggeration and claim that the real figure is about 350. Some of these deaths were also caused by secret South Vietnamese assassination squads who killed civilians who supported the NLF.

Whatever the real number, it is clear that the NLF had taken its chance to get rid of a large number of its enemies. This massacre helped the case of those in the United States and Saigon who claimed that many thousands more would die if the communists won. This is why the war had to go on.

B 150 United States troops were killed in the fighting to regain control of Hué from the Vietcong. Here troops are seen taking cover behind an American tank. The use of heavy weapons like tanks helps to explain why 60 per cent of Hué's houses were destroyed.

Military consequences

In military terms the Tet Offensive, which lasted less than a month, was a disaster for the Vietcong or NLF. Most of the 45 000 fighters killed were from the NLF and only a minority were from the North Vietnamese Army. American deaths came to 1500 and the ARVN lost 3000 dead. There were about 14 000 civilians killed. The offensive destroyed many of the finest fighters the Vietcong had and wiped out the NLF's organisation in the South.

These experienced southern communist leaders had to be replaced by men sent from the North. This meant that now the NLF was firmly under the control of the government in Hanoi. The NLF had finally lost its independence as a guerrilla organisation. Many resented the control of these northerners over 'their' movement.

C Huong Van Ba was an artillery officer in the NVA. He was involved in the Tet Offensive and told his American interviewer:

When the Tet campaign was over, we didn't have enough men left to fight a major battle, only to make hit-and-run attacks on posts. So many men had been killed that morale was very low. We spent a great deal of time hiding in tunnels, trying to avoid being captured. We experienced desertions and many of our people filtered back to their homes to join local guerrilla forces [instead of staying with the main NVA units]. We heard that in the North there were more young people trying to avoid the draft.

1 Why, in military terms, was the Tet Offensive a big risk for the Vietcong?
2 Look at source A.
   a) According to the map, who controlled or influenced most of South Vietnam?
   b) Why would the VC attacks on the towns shown come as such a shock to the South's government? (Clue: look where they are.)
   c) Does this map prove that the VC controlled or influenced most of the population of South Vietnam? Explain your answer. (Clue: Re-read the map caption.)
3 Why could it be said that the executions carried out by the VC in Hué were a political mistake?
4 a) What, according to source C, were the main effects of the Tet Offensive on the communist forces? (Think about morale in the North and the South and casualties.)
   b) Cross-referencing sources is a useful way to decide how reliable a source is. If it is supported by other evidence, it is more likely to be reliable. Are the views of source C supported by the rest of the evidence in this chapter?

The Tet Offensive and the Media

Did the media affect the outcome of the war?

To begin with, the United States newspaper and television journalists (the media) were in favour of the war. The chief editor of *Life* magazine in 1965 wrote that 'the war is worth winning'. Gradually, though, attitudes began to change. Two years later, that same editor wrote in October 1967 that the United States was not really threatened by the communists in Vietnam and that the war was not worth the lives of young Americans.

The credibility gap widens

In December 1966 the North Vietnamese finally permitted an American journalist to visit North Vietnam. Harrison Salisbury was from the respected *New York Times*. He reported on the destruction to civilian areas and the many civilian casualties caused by American bombing raids.

The United States military had always denied that their bombs hit civilian targets. If there were civilian casualties, they claimed, then there weren't many of them. The journalist's reports widened still further the 'credibility gap'. This is the difference between what the American military and government said and what the American people believed. The wider the gap, the less the people believed.

By 1968 the United States military in Vietnam had become very suspicious of the role of the American media. They were convinced that they were turning public opinion in the United States against a war that the American and South Vietnamese forces were winning. The commander of the forces in Vietnam, General Westmoreland, had claimed in 1967 that he could see the light of victory at the end of the tunnel.

It is more likely that journalists were only reflecting a change of opinion among the people of the United States. In August 1967, for the first time, an opinion poll showed that more Americans (46 per cent) thought the war was a 'mistake' than those (44 per cent) who thought it was right. It's worth pointing out, though, that this poll was taken just after President Johnson had announced an increase in taxes to pay for the war. The war was costing Americans $20 billion a year at this time.

'That's about all there is to say right now. The next time you hear from me, it'll probably be in person. I've got less than two months left in Vietnam.' Letter from Sergeant George Storz. He was killed a month later.

A General Westmoreland commanded the United States forces in Vietnam until June 1968. In 1979 he gave his views on the role of the American media in the war. He believed that news coverage of the war gave North Vietnam the message that the United States lacked the will to win the war:

> Actions by opponents of the war in the United States were supported by the news media. The media, no doubt, helped to back up the message that the war was 'illegal' and 'immoral' …
>
> Then came the enemy's Tet Offensive of early 1968. The North Vietnamese and the Vietcong suffered such a military defeat that it took them four years to recover. Despite this, reporting of the offensive by press and television in the United States gave an impression of an endless war that could never be won.

B A 15-man VC suicide squad fought its way into the American embassy in Saigon. Within six hours they were all dead, like the ones shown here. But the political effect of this daring attack was much more important than the military result.

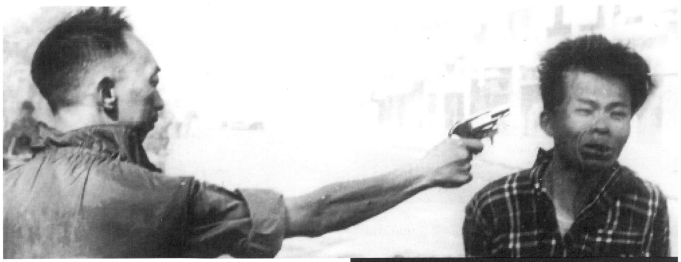

The impact of Tet

The news film of the Tet Offensive had a dramatic effect. Especially stunning was film of the Vietcong guerrillas fighting in the grounds of the United States embassy. Walter Cronkite, America's most respected television journalist, saw the news film. 'What the hell is going on? I thought we were winning this war,' he said. Cronkite's opinion would influence millions of Americans. 'If I've lost Walter, I've lost Mr Average Citizen,' President Johnson said.

The next day saw the most dramatic television film of the offensive and perhaps the war. An American news cameraman filmed a tied-up VC suspect being led by a group of ARVN troops. As he was filming, the Chief of the Saigon Police walked up to the suspect and took out his pistol. He shot him once in the head. The VC suspect collapsed to the ground, a fountain of blood gushing from the side of his head.

To American television viewers, the incident was shocking. The Chief of Police had clearly shot the

D This photograph is probably the most dramatic picture of the entire war. 'Buddha will understand,' said the Chief of Police after the execution. Buddha may have done but the American public didn't. To them, it looked like the execution of a man who hadn't even been tried. He was, though, a member of the Vietcong.

man without a trial, on the spot, and not in self-defence. To viewers the victim was just a man wearing a check shirt and shorts. Was this the sort of behaviour the United States was defending in Vietnam?

C The American historian, Stanley Karnow, wrote this about the role of the media during the war:

But public opinion surveys conducted at the time made it plain that the Tet episode scarcely altered American attitudes toward the war.

Public 'support' for the war had been slipping steadily for two years before Tet. This was a trend caused by the increasing casualties, rising taxes and, especially, the feeling that there was no end in view. For a brief moment after the Tet offensive began, Americans rallied behind the flag in a predictable display of patriotic fervour. But their mood of despair quickly returned as the fighting dragged on, and their support for the conflict continued to fall.

1 How did the attitude of the media to the war change after Harrison Salisbury's visit to the North in December 1966?
2 a) What was 'the credibility gap'?
   b) Why was it so serious for the United States government?
3 a) Why would a historian consider source A to be especially valuable? (Clue: think about its provenance.)
   b) Do you think source A's provenance makes it more or less reliable as evidence about America's role in the war?
4 a) In what way is source C's view different from source A?
   b) What reasons can you give to explain this difference?
5 'The Tet Offensive was a military victory for the United States but a political defeat.' Using the sources in this chapter and your own knowledge, explain whether you agree or disagree with this interpretation.

The Soldiers' War

What was it like to fight in Vietnam? What were the effects of American bombing? What was morale like on each side?

Statistics

Around 2.8 million Americans served in Vietnam. Two million of them were drafted or conscripted. But only about ten per cent of these were likely to see any combat. In a typical 12-month tour of duty, the average GI (United States soldier) stood a two per cent chance of being killed and a ten per cent chance of getting seriously wounded. The casualty rate is much higher, though, if you consider only those who took part in actual combat.

Of all those killed in combat, 43 per cent died in the first three months of their tour of duty. Only six per cent of deaths took place among soldiers in their last three months. In total, 58 000 were killed. Their average age was 19. If you were white, wealthy, and well educated you stood a much better chance of not being drafted. Those who had places at university could have their call-up delayed until after their degree. For this reason, blacks, Hispanics (Americans of Mexican descent) and poor whites made up the majority of the infantry in Vietnam.

To begin with most of the men who arrived in the very early stages of the war were professional soldiers. The army was their chosen career. They were motivated and committed. By 1967, however, most of the arrivals had been drafted. Very few believed that they were defending democracy or even cared. Their only aim was to count the day to DEROS (Date Eligible for Return from Overseas).

Training: 'Kill a gook every day'

The Americans were trained to see their enemy as less than human. It made it easier to kill them. Slang terms for the NVA, Vietcong or even just the Vietnamese were an important part of this. 'Gook', 'dink' and 'slope'(from the shape of the eyes of the Vietnamese) were common terms.

B One soldier remembered his training in the Marines:

We didn't look at the Vietnamese as human beings. They were subhuman. To kill them would be easy for you. If you continued with this process … you didn't have any bad feelings about it because they were a subhuman species. That was how they prepared us for it.

They used the terms 'gooks' and 'zipperheads' and we had to kill different insects every day and they would say, 'There's a gook, step on it and squash it,' and similar things like that. Every day you had to kill something. And they kept putting that in your mind. These were gooks and you had to kill them.

'Cherries'

Westmoreland hoped that the one-year tour of duty system would keep up morale. This was probably not true. The constant supply of replacements undermined morale. Replacements were the new arrivals, brought in to replace men who had been killed or severely wounded. It wasn't easy joining a group of men who had been buddies for many months and had seen combat together. It would take a few weeks before replacements, known as 'cherries', would be accepted. Cherries made mistakes and on a patrol a mistake could cost the lives of other men. Most would not be accepted until they had been tested under combat conditions.

The most unpopular jobs in an infantry platoon of 35 men were operating either the radio or the M-60 machine-gun. Both were three times heavier than a rifle and the men carrying them were

A A wounded GI is being taken back for medical treatment during the battle for Hué in 1968. American and communist troops tried very hard to bring back the bodies of their dead. This was good for morale. The VC and NVA also did this because it added to the United States troops' frustration as a high 'body count' of enemy dead was a key part of the American strategy.

certain targets in an ambush. Even though they were unpopular jobs, they were never given to inexperienced soldiers. Walking point was also unpopular. It involved leading the platoon in the forest, watching for the enemy and checking for booby traps.

As you might expect, soldiers feared death and being wounded. But in some cases they feared being a coward even more. Nobody liked to show himself up in front of his buddies.

C A soldier remembers his first battle:

Oh God, I was so damn scared! My stomach was churning. I suspected I was going to vomit and also have a bowel movement at the same time. I remember thinking I would rather throw up because that wouldn't show, but I can also remember - and why a person would think about that at a time like that - but I thought, God, I don't want to mess my pants. If they find me and see that I've messed my pants they are going to know how scared I was.

Fifty-one per cent of Americans killed in the war were killed by small arms fire. Small arms are pistols, rifles and machine-guns – basic military equipment. It was not a war of big battles, involving thousands of troops but a war of small, deadly skirmishes or 'fire-fights', often during ambushes. These would involve only a few dozen men on each side, fighting at close range.

Booby traps

Soldiers out on patrol didn't only have an enemy ambush to worry about. Eleven per cent of deaths were caused by booby traps. These were cheap, easy to make, and very effective. Sharpened bamboo stakes, hidden in shallow pits under sticks and leaves, could easily pierce the sole of a boot. Sometimes the spikes were smeared with human or animal excrement so the wound was infected. A trip wire strung across a jungle path would pull a grenade out of a tin can when it caught a soldier's leg. Soldiers wading in deep water could also catch the trip wire on these traps.

Mines were more sophisticated traps. A soldier would trigger off a 'Bouncing Betty' mine by stepping on it. The mine was fired about a metre into the air before exploding in front of the man walking behind. It was designed to explode at the same height as a man's genitals. The casualties caused by these weapons greatly increased the tension and frustration the survivors felt because there was no enemy to be seen, no one to shoot at. Some mines were made from unexploded bombs.

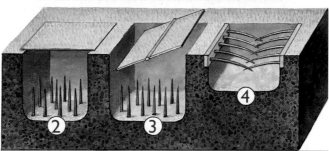

D Booby traps were designed to maim or kill careless American soldiers. Punji stakes made from bamboo were dug in on the other side of a trip wire (1). Pits (2) and (3) were as deep as a man, trap (4) was designed to snare a man's lower leg (the curved spikes made it difficult to pull their leg out).

E One infantryman remembered the effect of one of these mines:

Pulaski tripped a booby trap and it blew the hell out of him. Evidently, the enemy stole some of our explosives or something. The explosion blew one leg off about midway between the knee and the groin, and the other leg was blown off at the calf ... The explosion left his body naked. His testicles were gone and his penis was just barely attached.

---

1 Can you suggest a reason why so many more soldiers were killed in their first three months of duty?

2 Why do you think replacements were never given the job of operating the platoon machine-gun or radio?

3 Why do you think 'walking point' was another unpopular job?

4 What, according to source B, was the purpose behind training?

5 a) What evidence can you find in this chapter to support the idea that the Vietnam War was really fought with just basic military technology?

   b) The VC were particularly good at making their own simple but deadly weapons. Why was this an advantage for them?

DEATH FROM THE AIR

What the North Vietnamese and the Vietcong feared most were the bombing raids by American planes. The communist forces dug deep tunnels and used these as air-raid shelters. The tunnels around Saigon ran for 320 kilometres (see source A). Not all tunnels, though, were as well-designed as these. Some offered little protection from the effect of the bombs – at least for the men, as Source B makes clear.

C NVA medical units learned to operate underground by the light of oil lamps in terrible conditions, as one female nurse remembered:

> I was inexperienced, and my first sight and smell of blood and pus made me so sick that I vomited and couldn't work. Some of the wounded had lost arms or legs. Or their bellies had been ripped open by bomb fragments, and their intestines were spilling out. Others were horribly burned by napalm. Many, who had been lying in the jungle for days, were brought in with maggots crawling out of their infected wounds.

The Americans had developed a variety of bombs for use against the enemy. All of them caused terrible wounds. Cluster bombs were called 'mother bombs' by the Vietnamese. They exploded in the air and released up to 600 smaller bombs. When one of these hit the ground, it exploded into thousands of metal pellets.

Conical air raid shelter

Concealed trap door · Sleeping chamber · Conference chamber · Punji stake trap · 'Dien Bien Phu' kitchen · Remote smoke outlet

Firing post

False tunnel

Ventilation shaft

Aid station for wounded · Tunnel drop as blast wall · Blast- gas- and waterproof trap doors · Well · Storage space for weapons, explosives and rice

Water table

A A VC tunnel system.

B One Vietcong fighter remembered the effect of the bombing:

> Even when there weren't direct hits, the pressure from the explosions would kill people in their bunkers. For some reason, men were killed more easily by concussions than women. Female guerrillas would often survive attacks that killed men who were in the same bunkers. We didn't know why, but we had a theory that men's testicles were especially vulnerable to pressure. Whatever the reason, we learned to make bunkers with two openings instead of one, so that the pressure inside would be able to escape.

D Two innocent victims of an accidental bombing raid on a South Vietnamese village. The napalm has burnt the skin from these children's bodies. Shreds hang loose. They both died.

These bombs could kill but they were really intended to wound. A wounded enemy has to be given medical treatment. He has to be taken from the battlefield by other soldiers. All this ties up other troops and scarce medical resources. Later the pellets were made from fibre glass. These pellets didn't show up in X-rays and so operations were more difficult.

Napalm was a bomb which explodes and showers the surrounding victims with a burning petroleum jelly. Napalm sticks to the skin and burns at 800 degrees centigrade.

E A United States pilot tells of the effects of bombing with napalm:

> The original napalm bomb wasn't so hot – if the gooks were quick they could scrape it off. So the boys started adding polystyrene – now it really sticks. But then if the gooks jumped under water it stopped burning, so they started adding white phosphorous so as to make it burn better. It'll even burn under water now. And one drop is enough, it'll keep on burning right down to the bone so they die anyway from phosphorous poisoning.

'Fragging'

The men in each platoon found it difficult to get to know each other and to work as a unit. No sooner had the men learned the skills of survival and combat than it was time for them to leave. Soldiers getting close to the end of their tour (being 'short') were desperate to avoid combat or take risks. This made them less effective. One commentator wrote that 'America did not fight a ten-year war, it fought a one-year war ten times.' The one-year tour of duty system probably greatly reduced the fighting efficiency of the American army.

Relations between officers and conscripted soldiers could become very difficult. Many officers were career soldiers. They wanted promotion and needed a successful combat record with a high body count of enemy 'kills'. Most of the ordinary GIs simply wanted to stay alive until their DEROS. Hostility to these officers sometimes led the men to kill them. 'Fragging' was the term used to describe the killing of an officer by his own men. The estimate is that three per cent of all officers who died in Vietnam were killed by their own troops. During 1970 and 1971 there were over 700 cases of fragging in the United States army and this was when there were fewer troops in Vietnam.

F Soldiers who informed the authorities about massacres or ill-treatment of the civilian population took a risk. The soldier in this source knew it was a difficult decision to make.

> There was one guy in the platoon that told me they were searching in this hut one time and there was a really pretty, young Vietnamese girl. He walked over to her and jammed his hands down her pants and started to take her clothes off. She was shivering and scared. There were two or three guys in the hut. The girl's mother came in and started raising all kinds of hell and they backed off. I had the feeling that they would have raped her if her mother hadn't come in.
>
> I don't know what I would have done if I had been faced with that sort of thing. I don't think I would have taken part in it, but I also don't think I would have tried to stop it. That would have been encouraging your own sudden death. These are the guys who get in fire fights with you. It would have been too easy to get blown away.

Drugs

Drug taking further reduced the effectiveness of United States forces in Vietnam. Marijuana was the most popular drug. GIs would smoke it in base camp and during 'R and R'. R and R was Rest and Recreation, a period of leave away from the front line. Cocaine and heroin were also used. Amphetamines were used to keep troops awake during night-time ambushes and just to get 'high'. In 1971 5000 men were treated in hospital for combat wounds and 20 000 for drug abuse.

'The whole war was a sham. There was no moral purpose, it was a fraud.' Oliver Stone, film director, 1987.

1 Can you think of a reason why tunnels would be especially useful for ambushes?
2 What evidence is there in source C to support the idea that bombing had a terrible effect on the communist forces?
3 What do you suppose the soldier in source F meant by 'It would have been too easy to get blown away'?
4 The soldier in source F believed he might have been killed by his own side if he had tried to stop the abuse of the young girl. Can you suggest any other reasons why soldiers in such situations stand by or even get involved in crimes like these?

WHAT WAS MORALE LIKE ON EACH SIDE?

The fact that American troops used drugs and sometimes 'fragged' their own officers suggests low morale among them. Other factors can also lead to low morale. Soldiers need to believe that the cause they are fighting for is a good one. They also need to believe that the people back home support the war and their part in it. If they believe the cause isn't good or that they're not supported, then troops quickly lose heart. Between 1966 and 1973 there were 503 000 incidents of desertion in the American army in Vietnam. It should be pointed out, though, that this doesn't mean that 503 000 *different* soldiers deserted.

The morale of American troops seemed to be good in the early stages of the war. This may have been because most of these men were full-time, career soldiers and had volunteered. As the war went on, more and more of the troops were conscripted ones. Many of these did not want to be there.

There was also racial tension between black and white troops. But the effect of this is hard to judge. Source B suggests that relations between black and white soldiers depended on where they were. What mattered was whether they were in the 'bush' where combat was likely or in the 'rear' where the men were mostly safe.

A A wounded white soldier is helped from the field by a black GI in 1968. Relations between black and white troops at the frontline were generally good. But, back in the United States, blacks often saw the war from a different point of view. 'The Vietcong never called us nigger' ran one protest banner from an anti-war demonstration by black veterans of the war. What point were the protesters making?

B One marine recalled that blacks in Vietnam in the late 1960s:

> ... banded together, wore slave bracelets [braided from boot laces] ... and referred to whites as 'the beast' ... Blacks gave each other 'the power' [or dap], a complicated series of handclasp-handshake movements, as a greeting. From a distance, or just walking by, two blacks always gave each other the raised fist salute. 'Give me some power, Bro – been bleedin' for the beast.' Whites would laugh and talk about it behind their backs and trouble was always seething beneath the surface.
>
> But in the bush we needed each other so much that we got along pretty well. The rear was a different story ... The farther back in the rear you got, the worse it was. And blacks and whites who were friends in the bush felt intimidated or awkward together in the rear.

C An American infantryman discussed why they were fighting with a journalist in October 1971:

> The only thing you fightin' for is your own life. You fightin' to go back home, and you got fight your way out of here. You can't go out there and just give it up. You fight for yourself, man. I'm fighting to go home.

Communist morale

Most commentators on the war at the time felt that the morale of the Vietcong and North Vietnamese troops was much better. There is plenty of evidence from GIs which tells of fierce resistance and fighting to the death by communist forces. The general impression is that the communists were almost superhuman and could not be beaten. Not all the evidence supports this view.

D This extract is taken from a letter from an NVA soldier to his girlfriend in South Vietnam, dated 10 July 1971:

> This terrible war makes so many strange thoughts race through my head. I would like to jump up thousands of miles to get away from here, from killing. Before, I did not know what it was to kill a man; now that I have seen it, I don't want to do it any more. But it is the duty of a soldier to die for his country, me for our fatherland, the enemy for his. There is no choice.

E A North Vietnamese artillery officer told his American interviewer how the Tet Offensive (1968) affected morale among his men:

When the Tet campaign was over, we didn't have enough men left to fight a major battle, only to make hit-and-run attacks on posts. So many men had been killed that morale was very low. We spent a great deal of time hiding in tunnels, trying to avoid being captured. We experienced desertions …

F Soldiers didn't just fight in the jungles. Here black and white GIs make their way through a town in South Vietnam. Tensions between black and white troops were not helped by the fact that in 1965 24 per cent of US troops killed were black – but they only made up ten per cent of the population of the USA.

Q

1 What issues affect the morale of soldiers in combat?
2 Why does source B suggest that relations between black and white soldiers depended on where they were?
3 a) What is the difference in attitude to the war between source C and source D?
   b) What effect do you think this would have had on the way the war was fought?
4 a) In what ways does source E give a different impression of NVA morale?
   b) Is there anything in the provenance of sources D and E which might explain this difference? (Look carefully at the dates and where the sources come from.)

Extended writing
'The morale of the American troops in Vietnam got worse the longer the war went on.' What is your opinion of this view? The following points may help you to answer:

- differences between professional and conscript soldiers;
- what each side was fighting for;
- 'fragging' – drugs – race;
- tour of duty system;
- enemy tactics.

Crisis at Khe Sanh

The early months of 1968 were very tense ones for American forces in Vietnam. The Tet Offensive came as a dramatic and unwelcome surprise. Up in the north of South Vietnam another battle was taking place which also gripped the attention of the American people.

A week before the Tet Offensive, on 21 January 1968, the North Vietnamese Army began an 11-week siege of an American military base. Six thousand United States and ARVN troops were surrounded in their base at Khe Sanh by about 20 000 NVA troops. The North Vietnamese began the attack because they knew the Americans would do everything to defend the base. This would force the United States military to take troops, supplies and aircraft away from the cities to help the defenders. This is exactly what the NVA wanted to help their Tet Offensive.

'A shell came right into this man's trench and what they had to send home would probably fit inside a handkerchief.' Anonymous marine at Khe Sanh.

Not another Dien Bien Phu

Some journalists at the time compared the situation of the surrounded base at Khe Sanh to Dien Bien Phu in 1954. Here a French base was also surrounded by the enemy. The base was captured and France quit the war. Westmoreland was determined the same would not happen to Khe Sanh. Nor was it likely to happen. Unlike the French, the United States forces had large numbers of artillery, helicopters and aircraft to use in their defence of the base.

Aircraft kept the base supplied and dropped a devastating tonnage of bombs on the communist forces. The NVA around Khe Sanh was the most heavily bombed target in the history of warfare. By the middle of April, United States ground troops had fought their way through to the base and the siege was over. The NVA forces retreated. The result was that perhaps as many as 10 000 NVA troops had been killed in the siege for the deaths of just 500 Americans and South Vietnamese. In this sense, the battle for Khe Sanh was clearly a victory for the United States. On the other hand, two months later the Americans abandoned the base and withdrew.

My Lai – a different kind of war

On 16 March 1968, just south of Khe Sanh, an American patrol approached a small village called My Lai. The battle for Khe Sanh and the Tet Offensive were still raging. Lieutenant Calley and his platoon, searching for VC, entered the village. They then committed the worst, reported American atrocity of the war. An American investigation into the massacre later reported that 347 men, women, children and babies were murdered. Some of the women had been raped first. Other reports put the number of dead at over 500.

A This is an ADSID — Air-Delivered Seismic Intrusion Detector. Despite its clumsy title, these effective devices detected movement and warned Americans that enemy troops were approaching. The metre-long spikes dug into the ground as the ADSIDs were dropped from planes. The Americans used hundreds around Khe Sanh.

The radio operator ... then stepped within two feet of the boy and shot him in the neck with a pistol. Blood gushed from the child's neck. He then tried to walk off, but he could only take two or three steps. Then he fell onto the ground. He lay there and took four or five deep breaths and then he stopped breathing. The radio operator turned to Stanley and said, 'Did you see how I shot that son of a bitch?' Stanley told Carter, 'I don't see how anyone could just kill a kid.'

... Le Tong, a 28-year-old rice farmer, reported seeing one woman raped after GIs killed her children. Nguyen Khoa, a 37-year-old peasant, told of a 13-year-old girl who was raped before being killed. GIs then attacked Khoa's wife, tearing off her clothes. Before they could rape her, however, Khoa said, their six-year-old son, riddled with bullets, fell and saturated her with blood. The GIs left her alone.

Impact of My Lai

News of the massacre was kept quiet. Officially, the operation at My Lai had been a success. United States troops had killed 90 VC fighters, according to the company commander's report. The only casualty the Americans had was one soldier shot in the foot. This soldier (Carter in source B) later said he had shot himself to get out of the killing.

But eventually, in November 1969, the American press got hold of the story from a soldier who had heard rumours of the massacre. Calley, as the officer in charge of one of the platoons, was the only soldier convicted of murder after the investigation. In 1971 he was sentenced to life imprisonment for personally killing 22 villagers. He served three-and-a-half years before President Nixon pardoned him and he became a free man.

The killings at My Lai divided the United States. Some defended Calley and his men because they were fighting for their country. They believed that the villagers had been helping the Vietcong and that there were VC in the village. In one poll, 49 per cent refused to believe the report at all. When photographs of the dead (see source D) were published in an American newspaper, there were

complaints that the paper was 'rotten and anti-American'. Others claimed that it showed how rotten the war was and that My Lai was just one of many other massacres that nobody knew about. Many believed that the Army should have put on trial Calley's superior officers as well.

Americans were used to seeing themselves as the 'good guys'. Some now wondered how true this was if their soldiers were responsible for massacres like My Lai.

D A few of the 500 or so villagers murdered by American troops at My Lai. Not all Americans were horrified by the massacre.

1 Why was the timing of the attack on Khe Sanh so important to the North Vietnamese?
2 What evidence is there in the text that the base at Khe Sanh was not really vital for the Americans?
3 What evidence is there in the text and the sources that not all the troops at My Lai supported the killings?
4 My Lai divided the American people. Explain why:
   a) some supported the soldiers involved in the killings;
   b) some became more opposed to the war.
5 'My Lai was not the fault of Calley and his men. It was the fault of the way they had been trained.' Using your own knowledge (see chapter 11) and the sources, explain whether you agree or disagree with this interpretation.

Opposition to the War in the United States

In what ways did people oppose the war? Why did opposition increase?

'Hey, Hey, LBJ, How Many Kids You Kill Today?' Chant of anti-war demonstrators.

You will have read in Chapter 10 how the media began to question the war in 1967. By this date, also, a national movement against the war had developed. Opposition came from a variety of political points of view. Some were socialists or radicals who sympathised with the struggle of the people of Vietnam to create an independent and unified Vietnam. Others were pacifists who were against the war on moral and religious grounds. They believed that all war is wrong and that this one in particular was against Christian teaching. There were also those who simply felt that Vietnam wasn't worth the lives of young American men.

A An anti-war demonstration in front of the Pentagon in October 1967. The large placard shows a picture of President Johnson over the words 'War criminal'. Growing opposition to the war helped to convince Johnson that he would not be re-elected as president in 1968.

Burning draft cards

An early form of protest was draft card burning. Men who were to be conscripted or drafted into the army received a draft card from one of 4000 draft boards. Some burned their draft orders in public. Others just refused to report for training. Both were criminal offences. By the end of 1969 there were 34 000 draft-dodgers wanted by the police. Many crossed the border to Canada to avoid arrest.

Other opposition groups took to raiding draft board offices and burning their records. This is what happened in Catonsville, Maryland in May, 1968. Two of the nine people involved were Catholic priests and another was a former nun. They were all imprisoned. In Milwaukee protesters burned 10 000 files.

At first the prison sentences were very harsh. One of the 'Catonsville Nine' was sentenced to six years in prison for an earlier attack. But the sentences began to get shorter. The 'Camden 28' took part in the last attack on a draft board in 1971. They were all found not guilty in 1973.

Students were involved in the anti-war movement from the beginning. The Student Non-violent Coordinating Committee had been set up to campaign for equal rights for blacks but in 1966 it also began to oppose the war. A year later in April 1967, the black civil rights leader, Martin Luther King, joined the anti-war movement (see source B). He was worried that the poor made up most of the recruits to Vietnam and that poor blacks were a big part of these.

B Martin Luther King speaks out against the war:

We were taking the young black men who had been ruined by our society and sending them 8000 miles away to defend freedom in South East Asia – a freedom which they had not found in their own country, in places like South West Georgia and East Harlem. Instead, we have repeatedly seen the cruel image of Negro and white boys on TV screens as they kill and die together for a nation that has been unable to provide schools in which Negro and white children can sit together.

Luther King was disappointed with the failure of President Johnson's 'Great Society' programme. When Johnson won the 1964 election he promised a 'Great Society' in which the poor, and especially blacks, would receive decent welfare payments and decent homes. However, little had been achieved. Johnson wanted these improvements but the government couldn't afford them and the war. The war was costing over $20 billion a year and Johnson had to cut something. The Great Society was put aside.

> **C** In a book written about him in 1976 after his retirement, President Johnson explained his reasons for abandoning his Great Society programme:
>
> I knew from the start that … if I abandoned the Great Society in order to get involved with that bitch of a war on the other side of the world, then I would lose everything at home. All my programs. All my hopes to feed the hungry and shelter the homeless. All my dreams to provide education and medical care to the browns and the blacks and the lame and the poor. But if I left that war and let the Communists take over South Vietnam, then I would be seen as a coward and my nation would be seen as one which gave in to threats. We would both find it impossible to achieve anything for anybody anywhere on the entire globe.

Johnson quits

In March 1968 Johnson announced that he would not stand for re-election as president in November. He realised that the war would cost him any chance of being re-elected. Some would oppose Johnson because they would blame him for not winning the war. Others would oppose him because he was going on with it. Earlier that same month, Robert McNamara, the Secretary of Defence since 1961, announced that he would be quitting politics. He said that the bombing of North Vietnam was not working and should be stopped.

Developments like these encouraged the anti-war movement. Huge protest marches against the war took place in 1969, 1970 and 1971. Perhaps as many as 500 000 took part in the protest in Washington in April 1971. Leading the way were Vietnam Veterans Against the War. Two weeks later there was a demonstration in support of the war. Only 15 000 took part.

Kent State

In April 1970 President Nixon, the president who replaced Johnson, announced that United States troops had entered neutral Cambodia. Nixon claimed that this was only to destroy communist bases used by the Vietcong. To opponents of the war, it just looked as though another 'Vietnam' was about to begin. Protests took place in universities across the United States at this escalation in their country's role. In one of these protests in May, four students were shot dead by National Guard soldiers at Kent State University, Ohio. The killings sparked off 400 protests and strikes in yet more universities.

D A student holds her head in shocked disbelief as she looks at the body of one of the four students shot dead at Kent State University.

1 Why do you think the authorities punished groups like the Catonsville Nine so severely?
2 Why, on the other hand, do you think that the Camden 28 were set free after their trial, five years later?
3 What do you suppose Martin Luther King in source B meant by the phrase that blacks were being sent across the world 'to defend freedom in South East Asia – a freedom which they had not found in their own country'?
4 What basic reason does Johnson in source C give for not getting out of Vietnam?
5 Martin Luther King opposed communism as much as Johnson did. How, then, do you explain why he had such a different view of the war from Johnson's?

WHY DID OPPOSITION INCREASE?

In 1971 more revelations about the war strengthened the growing opposition movement. One concerned details of a policy of assassination and torture carried out by the South Vietnamese under American supervision.

'Operation Phoenix'

In 1968 the United States Central Intelligence Agency (CIA) set up 'Operation Phoenix'. The purpose behind this was to identify and arrest VC suspects in areas controlled by the South Vietnamese government. The CIA set a target of 3000 suspects to be 'neutralised' each month. The idea was to arrest them, get them to talk, reveal other names and then imprison them. In the next three years secret South Vietnamese squads with American advisers captured and imprisoned 28 000 VC suspects. Another 20 000 were assassinated and 17 000 defected – that is, changed sides and supported the South.

The Phoenix programme was very controversial. Many of those taken had nothing to do with the Vietcong but were killed or imprisoned just to make up the quota for the month. Nonetheless, many of the victims were Vietcong. The murders and torture did cause a great deal of damage to the communist organisation in the South. Many of the NVA and VC forces escaped to Cambodia to get away from the assassination squads. In April 1970 Nixon sent United States troops after them into neutral Cambodia, seriously increasing the scale of the war.

Later, after the war, North Vietnamese and Vietcong leaders admitted that the Phoenix programme wiped out many communist bases in the South. But at the time details of the methods used by the Americans only strengthened the case of those who argued against the war. They argued that the methods used by the Phoenix programme showed that the war was a crime and the United States was acting criminally (see source B).

A A Vietcong suspect waits for 'questioning' during the Phoenix programme. Critics of the programme said that it was basically a terrorist campaign of assassination. It was, though, very effective in weakening the VC in South Vietnam.

B In December 1968 a military intelligence officer in South Vietnam gave evidence before Congress as to what happened when suspects were questioned under Phoenix:

A six-inch piece of round wood was inserted into one of my prisoner's ears and then tapped through the brain until he died. The starving to death in a cage of a Vietnamese woman who was suspected of being a part of the local VC political education group in one of the local villages ... the use of electronic gear such as sealed telephones attached to ... both the women's vagina and the men's testicles to shock them into giving information.

The Pentagon Papers

The second development which seriously damaged the reputation of the United States in 1971 was the 'Pentagon Papers'. The Pentagon is the headquarters of the United States Armed Forces. In 1967 Daniel Ellsberg, a Pentagon employee, was asked to collect together all the government documents to do with Vietnam from the 1940s onwards. There were 4000 pages of these. Ellsberg and others then added about 3000 pages of analysis of these documents. Together, they became known as the 'Pentagon Papers'.

These secret documents showed how United States government officials had sometimes lied about or covered up incidents in the war. Members of Congress were especially angry that important decisions to step up the war had been made without Congress being told. The documents also showed that United States governments had really failed to understand what they were getting involved in.

By 1969 Ellsberg had become an opponent of the war. He started to photocopy secretly all 7000 pages of the 'Pentagon Papers'. He passed the papers on to the *New York Times*. Ellsberg believed that the war was immoral. The United States was causing the deaths of many thousands of innocent civilians. He hoped the publication of the papers would help end the war. The *New York Times* started publishing them in June 1971.

President Nixon was unsure what to do. On the one hand, these papers were classified or secret documents which had been stolen. This was a criminal act. The papers also put the whole war in a very bad light. More people would now protest against it and his policy. On the other hand, the documents clearly showed the Kennedy and Johnson governments in a bad way. Both these men were Democrats and political opponents of Nixon's Republican party. The information in the papers would, therefore, damage the Democrats.

In the end, Nixon decided to try and stop all publication of the Pentagon Papers and to prosecute Ellsberg for theft and conspiracy. The **Supreme Court**, however, decided that the publication of the papers was not illegal and could continue. Charges against Ellsberg were dropped in 1973. Two earlier attempts to put Ellsberg on trial had to be stopped because Nixon had used illegal methods to get evidence against Ellsberg. These included bugging his telephone and breaking into his psychiatrist's office.

The release of the Pentagon Papers proved very harmful for Nixon – even though none of the documents had anything to do with his presidency. The publication of the papers made him more obsessed with security. He would now use any method, including criminal ones, to stop 'leaks' of information from the White House. This led him to use illegal methods to cover up the truth about the Watergate Scandal and forced him to resign in 1974.

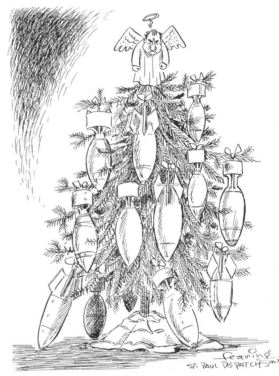

D Nixon, shown here as the angel on top of the Christmas tree, sometimes stopped bombing raids over North Vietnam during the Christmas period. This cartoonist clearly has his own view as to how genuine these gestures really were.

1 Why was Operation Phoenix so controversial?
2 Why could Operation Phoenix be described as a military success but a political failure?
3 Why was source B especially damaging for the United States? Think about both the content and provenance of the source.
4 What was so controversial about the Pentagon Papers?
5 The judge in source C believed that it is always wrong for a newspaper to publish stolen documents. Do you agree? Explain your answer.

Vietnamization and 'Peace'

How was a peace agreement achieved?

Nixon won the 1968 presidential election with a narrow majority over his Democrat opponent. One of the promises he made during the election campaign was to 'de-Americanize' the war. This suggested that the United States would play a smaller role in the war. But, the war would go on until 'peace with honour' could be achieved.

Peace talks with North Vietnam had started in Paris in May of 1968. No progress had been made. Each side stuck to its position. The biggest difference was the North would only agree to a peace which reunited both Vietnams. The United States would only agree to a peace which kept South Vietnam as a separate country.

The North also insisted that the communist National Liberation Front should form part of a new government in the South. The United States insisted that all North Vietnamese and American forces should leave South Vietnam. Then free elections could take place and the winners could set up a government. The Hanoi government believed that these elections would never be fair and rejected the American terms.

A The South Vietnamese Army, represented here as a scarecrow, was supposed to be able to fight the communists on its own after Vietnamization. The crows probably represent the NVA or VC forces.

Nixon developed a double strategy. He would carry out 'Vietnamization'. This meant that gradually American troops would leave Vietnam. As they left, the South Vietnamese Army would do more and more of the fighting. The United States would continue to support the Saigon government with the United States Air Force and equipment. At the same time, the peace negotiations in Paris would carry on. If the North refused to change its position, then the United States would increase the bombing raids on North Vietnam until they changed their minds.

There was only a small problem with this strategy. It didn't work. The Hanoi government realised that all it had to do was hang on. The anti-war movement in the United States was getting stronger each day. Eventually, the Americans would pull out of South Vietnam, leaving the South on its own. The ARVN would be no match for the communist forces and South Vietnam would be reunited with the North.

Thieu's fears

Nixon and his National Security adviser, Henry Kissinger, wanted a way out of the war without making it look as though the United States had lost. However, the South Vietnamese might oppose a settlement with Ho Chi Minh (who died in September 1969) or his successors. Nguyen Van Thieu had been president of South Vietnam since 1967. He was suspicious of the United States. One of Hanoi's terms was that Thieu could not be part of any new government of South Vietnam. Thieu was afraid that the Americans might dump him so as to reach an agreement with the North.

Nixon's solution was to negotiate directly with the North and leave out Thieu. Secret peace talks began in August 1969. While these talks went on, Nixon began to withdraw American troops from Vietnam. In April 1969, the number of United States soldiers in Vietnam reached its peak: 550 000. In June, Nixon announced that 25 000 of these would be coming home and he followed this up with another 35 000 in September.

Further invasions

The invasion of Cambodia (see page 33) achieved little in military terms and American troops withdrew after two months. Congress passed a law forbidding the use of American troops in either

Cambodia or Laos. Nixon had also hoped that the invasion of Cambodia would persuade Hanoi to be more flexible in negotiations. Instead, the North boycotted all talks – both the secret ones and the official negotiations in Paris – until American troops had pulled out of Cambodia.

US troops in Vietnam had dropped to 285 000. Nixon still believed that he could bully the North into making concessions. In February 1971 he approved a South Vietnamese invasion of Laos to block the Ho Chi Minh Trail. These ARVN forces were supported by American planes. The Americans had been bombing Laos since 1964 – secretly at first. But these were the first ground forces to enter the country. After six weeks the South Vietnamese troops withdrew, losing nearly 50 per cent killed or wounded. The failure of the ARVN proved to many that the South Vietnamese, on their own, could not stand up to the North Vietnamese. By the end of 1971 the Americans had just 140 000 men in Vietnam.

Peace agreement

By October 1972 Kissinger and the chief negotiator for North Vietnam, Le Duc Tho, had worked out a settlement. The terms were:

- a ceasefire over all Indo-China;
- American troops would withdraw from Vietnam within 60 days of the ceasefire;
- American prisoners of war would be freed – there were nearly 700 of these;
- elections would be held in the South to choose a new government;
- each side would stay only in those areas it controlled when the ceasefire started.

Kissinger was keen to get an agreement before Nixon stood for election in November. Nixon wanted a second term of four years as president and a peace agreement would clinch it. It did. Nixon won by a huge majority. Thieu, though, was furious. He believed, correctly, that the terms would leave the South at the mercy of the North. He rejected them. Le Duc Tho broke off further negotiations in December.

On 18 December 1972 Nixon ordered another massive bombing campaign over North Vietnam. In eleven days more bombs were dropped than in the whole of the period 1969 to 1971. As a gesture of Christian goodwill, the bombing was stopped for Christmas Day. The North agreed to re-open negotiations. Nixon told Thieu that if he didn't sign the agreement then the United States would sign it without him. Thieu gave in. The Paris Peace Agreement was signed on 27 January 1973.

B Many foreign papers were, like the American media, unhappy with Nixon's policy of talking peace at the same time as he stepped up the war. Here the British magazine, *Punch*, shows Nixon planting the American flag in a 'cliff-edge' Laos.

1 What was Vietnamization?
2 Suggest two ways in which the cartoonist in source A gets across the message that Vietnamization was not working.
3 How does the cartoonist in source B get across the idea that Nixon's invasion of Laos was a mistake?
4 Look at sources A and B, and source D from Chapter 13. What attitude do they all have in common to:
   a) the war?
   b) President Nixon?
5 In what ways might cartoons like these be useful to a historian of the Vietnam War?
6 'We have finally achieved peace with honour,' Nixon claimed on American television on 23 January. Explain whether you agree or disagree with his view.

Vietnam United

What happened after the Americans left?

The 'guests' of the 'Hanoi Hilton'

During the course of the war 839 Americans had been taken prisoner. A few managed to escape but 114 died as prisoners. By the end of March 1973 the North Vietnamese had handed over the remaining 691 to the United States. Many had been kept as prisoners in what they bitterly called the 'Hanoi Hilton'. Almost all of the prisoners were pilots shot down over North Vietnam on bombing raids. The communists considered these men to be war criminals and they were treated badly and, in some cases, tortured.

A An American pilot greets his family after being released in February 1973. Some had been prisoners since 1965.

On 29 March 1973 the last American troops left Saigon. For the United States the war was over. But not for the South. No one expected the ceasefire to hold. Indeed, Thieu already had plans for how he was going to break it. The South was in a good position in early 1973. The South Vietnamese, thanks to Nixon, had the world's fourth largest air force. Its army of one million men was

'We have finally stopped wasting lives in Vietnam. We must now stop wasting American dollars there too.' American senator, 1974.

equipped with the latest American weapons. Thieu's government controlled 75 per cent of South Vietnam and 85 per cent of its population.

'A house leaks from the roof'

The communists, on the other hand, were in a weak position. They were short of men, weapons, ammunition and food. Only in the autumn of 1973 did they feel strong enough to make small-scale attacks on the ARVN positions. Thieu had launched fairly successful attacks against the communists in the Mekong Delta and along the Cambodian border soon after the ceasefire. But the NVA and VC forces recaptured what they had lost by the spring of 1974.

The Army of the Republic of Vietnam was beginning to fall apart. ARVN morale was very poor. An American investigation in the summer of 1974 reported that 90 per cent of the South Vietnamese Army weren't being paid enough to support their families. Corrupt government officials were stealing the soldiers' pay. They insisted on bribes before handing over food and supplies. In desperation, ARVN officers squeezed the villagers for money to pay their men. This only led more peasants to support the VC. An old Vietnamese saying summed up well the situation: 'A house leaks from the roof.'

The speed of the South Vietnamese collapse surprised Hanoi. The North Vietnamese had plans to win the war in 1976 but they quickly brought these forward. By the middle of April 1975 NVA forces surrounded Saigon. Thieu complained that the Americans had broken their promise to provide enough aid to keep the South Vietnamese Army going. Congress had indeed cut back after the ceasefire on supplies to the South Vietnamese government.

But the South Vietnamese armed forces were not short of supplies. They had more than three times the number of artillery pieces and twice as many tanks as their communist enemy. They were short of commitment and leadership. On 25 April 1975, Thieu fled from South Vietnam to live in Great Britain. Several hundred thousand South Vietnamese who had reason to fear the communists were not so lucky.

The last 6000 Americans to leave Vietnam were lifted out of Saigon by helicopter on 30 April 1975. They left behind scenes of civilian panic.

B South Vietnamese who had worked for the Americans were desperately afraid of the North Vietnamese. They fought to get aboard aircraft which would fly them to safety. Here a South Vietnamese is punched in the face to get him off an already overcrowded plane.

The United States had directly employed 100 000 South Vietnamese during the war. These people feared the NVA would kill them for working with the enemy. They made desperate efforts to be taken out with their families but the United States only took with them a few thousand.

'You cannot give up what you do not have'

NVA troops entered the city on the same day. A tank broke down the gates of the South Vietnamese president's palace. A North Vietnamese colonel went up the steps of the palace. Inside, the President of South Vietnam was waiting for him. 'I have been waiting since early morning to hand over power to you', the President said. The NVA colonel's reply summed up the situation: 'You cannot give up what you do not have. You have nothing to fear. Between Vietnamese, there are no winners and no losers. Only the Americans have been beaten. If you love your country, then this is a moment of joy. The war for our country is over.'

For many others the war had been over a lot earlier than April 1975. One and a half million men, women and children had been killed. Of these, 660 000 NVA and Vietcong, and 223 000 South Vietnamese troops had died, along with 58 000 Americans. The other 587 000 dead were all civilians.

C For many the war would leave bitter memories as well as scars. But some, particularly on the communist side, would later look back on the war and see its better side. Tran Van Tra commanded the VC forces in South Vietnam:

> During the hard days of hunger and thirst we shared each piece of jungle root, each bit of firewood, each apple, each drink of spring water we had brought from the other side of the mountain. Every year on the Truong Son route [the Ho Chi Minh Trail] after months of exhaustion, we shared each spoonful of sugar or bit of salt, or offered each other the last anti-malaria tablet to help each other get to the final aim of freeing our country.

1 Why was the South still in a good position to win the war, even after the Americans left?
2 Why do you think the North Vietnamese considered American pilots to be war criminals?
3 Explain why the phrase 'A house leaks from the roof' is an accurate description of the situation in South Vietnam after the ceasefire.
4 'You cannot give up what you do not have.' What do you think the NVA colonel meant by this?
5 Look at source C. Many American soldiers felt the same way about the close friendships between 'buddies' during the war. Why, though, were they not likely to share exactly the same feelings as the VC commander in this source? (Clue: think about the hardships described and the 'final aim' of the VC.)

The Cold War and Beyond

How did the war affect relations between the superpowers? Why did China and Vietnam come into conflict?

You will remember from Chapter 3 that the United States first got involved in Vietnam because of its fear that communism was about to take over South East Asia. First the Americans supported the French against the Vietminh and then they got involved themselves. The United States knew that the Soviet Union and China were both supporting communist guerrilla groups in Vietnam and Malaya in the 1950s.

A Communist guerrilla groups were active almost everywhere in South East Asia during this period. From the United States' point of view, it looked as though the Soviet Union and China were determined to bring communists to power throughout the region.

Both communist powers hoped to spread their influence in the region at the expense of the United States. There was more communist activity in Thailand in the 1960s, and the Philippines in the 1970s. Communist groups actually took power in Cambodia and Laos in 1975 (see source A).

The domino theory

After the Korean War (1950–53), Vietnam was the only country where the United States could do something practical to stop the communists from toppling other South East Asian 'dominoes'. President Johnson didn't question the domino theory. United States governments in the 1950s and 1960s just assumed it was true.

So Vietnam became the Cold War front-line state of Asia in the same way that West Germany was in Europe. What the domino theory didn't explain was that no two communist movements in South East Asia were the same. Each communist movement had important *national* characteristics of its own.

At first glance, source A seems to support anti-communist fears. But the American State Department (foreign affairs) advisers failed to take into consideration a more important idea than communism. This was nationalism. Although communists in Vietnam, Laos, Cambodia and China shared the same communist beliefs, this did not stop them quarrelling with each other after they took power.

Traditional hostility between the Chinese and the Vietnamese was never far away. This was partly caused by the fact that the Chinese had once occupied Vietnam for 1000 years. It was made worse by China's behaviour at the Geneva Conference in 1954. Then, the Chinese forced the Vietminh to accept the division of Vietnam and at a point further north than the Vietminh wanted – the 17th parallel rather than the 13th.

However, these differences didn't surface until the late 1970s. Before then, the Soviet Union and China both provided important aid to North Vietnam – $300m worth in 1967. It suited both the Chinese and the Russians to see the United States bogged down in a bitter war in Vietnam. It also suited the Chinese – though they never said it at the time – to see the Vietnamese weakened by a long war. This would make it easier for China to influence events in South East Asia. Some years later, in 1981, the Prime Minister of Vietnam complained that the Chinese were 'always ready to fight to the last Vietnamese'.

Peaceful co-existence

On the other hand, the Russians didn't want the war to get out of hand. They tried hard to persuade the North Vietnamese to find a compromise with the United States. During the 1960s the Soviet Union favoured a policy of peaceful co-existence with the United States. This meant that the two rival superpowers should try to accept each other's existence and avoid confrontations.

The Chinese rejected this approach. The two communist powers, China and the Soviet Union, quarrelled over this in the early 1960s. They both tried to use North Vietnam as an ally against the other. The North Vietnamese skillfully played each power against the other to get the best for themselves. Once they had won the war in 1975, the North had to make a choice and they chose the Soviet Union.

Relations with the traditional enemy, China, became strained. The Vietnamese began to treat harshly those Vietnamese of Chinese origin who lived in Vietnam. This angered China and relations got sharply worse after 1978. In this year, the Vietnamese invaded Cambodia and overthrew the pro-Chinese communist government of Pol Pot. China was concerned by this growth in Vietnamese and, therefore, Soviet influence in the region. China's answer was to invade Vietnam in early 1979.

The Chinese suffered heavy casualties in the brief conflict. But they had made it clear that they wouldn't tolerate Vietnamese aggression in the region. In 1989 the Vietnamese ended their occupation of Cambodia and relations with China began to improve.

The end of the Cold War in the late 1980s between Russia and the United States meant that Soviet aid to Vietnam dried up. The Vietnamese were forced to improve relations with China because they could no longer rely on the backing of the former Soviet Union. This was even more the case when Russia ceased to be a communist state in 1991.

What all this proves is that the American State Department had got the situation wrong in the 1950s and 1960s. They believed that a reunited Vietnam would be a puppet state of the Chinese or the Soviet Union. In fact, Hanoi had no intention of allowing either of these communist powers to dominate Vietnam. If the Americans had understood a little better the people they fought, they would have realised that the Vietnamese are a fiercely independent people.

Nationalism, not communism, was the inspiration behind the resistance of the Vietnamese to the Japanese, the French and finally the Americans.

B This 1969 poster from communist Cuba is an example of the range of international support which the North Vietnamese received. It shows a NVA soldier in front of the North Vietnamese flag. Support for Ho Chi Minh from the world's communist nations helped to convince the United States that Vietnam was a key area of the Cold War.

1 Why was the United States so worried by events in South East Asia?

2 Why could it be said that neither the Soviet Union nor China really cared for the people of Vietnam?

3 What do you suppose the Vietnamese Prime Minister meant by the phrase that the Chinese were 'always ready to fight to the last Vietnamese'?

4 Why did the Vietnamese and Chinese eventually go to war with each other?

5 'The domino theory was wrong and led the United States into an unnecessary war in Vietnam.' Using the information in this chapter and your own knowledge, explain whether you agree or disagree with this interpretation. (Think about events in South East Asia after the war as well as before it.)

The War in Vietnam – Looking Back

Why did the United States lose the war? How did it affect the United States? How did it affect those who fought in it?

Hearts and minds

The Americans had realised from an early stage that the war could only be won by winning the support of the South Vietnamese peasants. This policy was called winning 'the hearts and minds' of the people. The problem was that the Americans didn't know how to do it and the rulers of South Vietnam didn't want to do it.

The key issue was land reform. The VC made sure that in areas under their control land was taken from the rich landowners and given to the poor peasants. This was very popular. Rulers of South Vietnam like Diem and Thieu would not carry out this policy and the Americans would not force them.

The Americans became more and more frustrated with their failure to break the support of the peasants for the VC. They tried the 'strategic hamlet' programme but that just caused even more resentment. In the end the Americans relied on purely military methods. They became frustrated because they couldn't tell VC supporters from ordinary villagers. This led to massacres like My Lai and increased the hatred of the peasants.

Tactics

The VC and NVA military strategy was as successful as their political one. They knew they couldn't match the massive firepower of the United States forces. So, they avoided large-scale battles and adopted guerrilla tactics instead. This wore down the American and ARVN forces which suffered casualties often without even catching a glimpse of their communist enemy.

The NVA and VC forces were never as well supplied or as well equipped as their opponents – until after 1973, anyway. But the Chinese and the Soviet Union provided enough weapons and supplies to keep the North Vietnamese going. Especially valuable were Soviet anti-aircraft guns, and missiles. Towards the end of the war Soviet tanks were important too.

Morale

Eventually, what really mattered was morale. The communist forces were much more committed to their cause and they fought with a real desire to win. The South Vietnamese Army was never a match in morale or fighting ability for the NVA and VC. The Americans could match the fighting ability of their enemies but they didn't have the same belief in their cause.

'Fragging' and drug abuse are examples of what happens to an army that has lost its way. News of the growing opposition movement to the war in the United States also undermined the troops' morale. This opposition was a big factor, too, in forcing an American withdrawal.

> 'Within the soul of each Vietnam veteran there is probably something that says, "Bad war, good soldier".' Vietnam veteran, 1982.

A The war in Vietnam would not have caused so many problems if all the Americans had been against it. But many were in favour of America's role as this 1968 demonstration supporting Johnson shows.

How did the war affect the United States?

The most immediate effect of the war was that President Johnson's ambitious 'Great Society' programme had to be abandoned (see Chapter 13). The cost of the war was too great to spend money on improved welfare. This meant that many of America's severe social problems – poverty, slums, lack of medical care for the poor, racial inequalities – could not be tackled.

The war bitterly divided the nation and caused protests and political conflict between supporters and opponents. It ruined Johnson's chances of being re-elected president in 1968 and even damaged Bill Clinton when he stood for the presidency in 1992. Clinton had been an opponent of the war at the time and he had avoided the draft.

It may be that after more than 20 years the war now causes fewer problems in the United States. But some of the effects of the war have remained. The Pentagon Papers proved that American governments had misled the people and even lied to them about the war. As a result, many Americans are much less willing to believe what their government tells them. The government won't win back the trust of these Americans that easily.

The Vietnam Syndrome

The long-term effects of the war have been just as important. For a long time the United States was determined to avoid fighting another 'Vietnam'. This meant that the Americans refused to send troops into any conflict which did not directly affect the United States' own security. This was known as the Nixon Doctrine. As a result, the United States did little to challenge *directly* the Soviet Union's actions in other countries such as Afghanistan and Angola. They were worried that American troops might get sucked into the conflict, as they had in Vietnam.

Eventually this concern that every international crisis was a potential Vietnam for the United States became less of a worry. Their decisive and speedy victory in the 1991 Gulf War ended the 'Vietnam Syndrome'. It allowed Americans to believe now that they could fight a war, win it quickly and with very few casualties.

Other problems, though, still remained. American soldiers returning to the United States may not have expected to be treated as heroes. But they certainly didn't expect to be treated as criminals or child murderers, as they sometimes were. Medical treatment for wounded or disabled veterans in the United States was poor. Many found it difficult to find jobs or to get their own jobs back – even though a government law made employers keep their jobs open for them.

More American veterans have committed suicide since the war than were killed in the war itself. For them, the process of adjusting to peace-time was too difficult. They felt betrayed by a country which was embarrassed by them.

An opinion poll in 1990 for *Time* magazine clearly showed the difference between the American public and the war veterans who had fought in the war. 57 per cent of the general public thought that the United States was wrong to get involved in the war while 58 per cent of veterans thought that the United States was right to get involved. Americans were embarrassed because they realised that Vietnam was not a 'good' war and because it was the first war the United States had ever lost.

B One former soldier remembered how the first thing he did after returning to the United States was to get a drink in the airport bar. There some young people of his age – 19 or 20 – spoke to him:

'You just got back from where?,' one of the kids says.

'Vietnam.'

'How do you feel about killing all of those innocent people?' the woman asks me out of nowhere.

I didn't know what to say. The bartender got a little uptight. But, I didn't say anything. They told me when I got discharged from the army that I was going to get this hassle. But, I didn't believe them.

'Excuse me,' I called the bartender over. 'Could I buy them all a drink?' I felt guilty. I did kill. I tried to make up for it somehow.

'We don't accept any drinks from killers,' the girl says to me.

---

1 What did winning 'the hearts and minds' of the South Vietnamese peasants mean?
2 What specific reason does the text give for the failure of the Americans to win over these 'hearts and minds'?
3 Can you suggest a reason why:
   a) Soviet tanks weren't much use to the VC and NVA forces in the years before 1973?
   b) Soviet tanks were more useful after 1973?
4 Why did American veterans feel so bitter after they returned to the United States?

COMING TO TERMS WITH VIETNAM

Hollywood's treatment of the Vietnam War has reflected the way Americans feel about it. The only film to be made about the war while it was still going on was *The Green Berets*. The United States Army enthusiastically co-operated with the film's director and star – John Wayne. The army also had control over the script. The film made a respectable profit but it was laughed at by the film critics. It was really a western. Wayne and his Special Forces team were the cowboys and the brutal, murdering Vietcong were the Red Indians. John Wayne's enthusiasm for playing the war hero was, perhaps, intended to make up for the fact that he managed to avoid serving in the United States Army during the Second World War between 1941 and 1945.

A *Born on the Fourth of July* was based on the real experience of a Vietnam veteran, played by Tom Cruise. He was paralysed in the war and became disgusted by the poor medical treatment given to disabled veterans. He joined the anti-war protest movement. But his reaction was not typical. 61 per cent of veterans in a 1990 poll said they were proud of their role in the war.

The films which came after the war were very different. Films like *Platoon* (1986), *Full Metal Jacket* (1987), and *Hamburger Hill* (1987) left out the sentimental heroics of *The Green Berets* to give a more honest and bloody view of the war. Oliver Stone, the director of *Platoon*, fought in the war. In 1976 he wrote a script for the film but none of the major Hollywood film studios would agree to make it. Stone's view of the war was too bleak and depressing. It wasn't until 1986 that he found the money to begin work on the film. The US army, though, refused to offer help in the making of it.

By 1987 the Cold War between the United States and Russia was beginning to fade. All the same, the old attitudes died hard. In 1987 *Pravda*, the official paper of the Communist Party in Russia, pointed out how Stone had been turned down by the Hollywood studios to get money to make his film. *Pravda* claimed the reason was because *Platoon* didn't show the American troops as heroes. Its view of the war, the paper said, was too gloomy and realistic for Hollywood. 'The film,' *Pravda* concluded, 'calls out that war is terrible and that an unjust war is a hundred times more terrible.'

The Vietnam War – the Bill

The financial cost of the war was easy to add up. Its social cost has been more difficult to judge. Many Americans shared *Pravda's* view that the war was unjust. Those who had protested against the Vietnam War became more confident about challenging the policies of their government. Once the war was over they continued their protests. Now their target was America's nuclear weapons. President Reagan (1981–89) gave them plenty to protest about. He spent vast sums of money on modernising the Unites States' nuclear weapons system. The Vietnam War cost the United States $120 billion. Some of this money would normally have been spent on up-dating America's nuclear weapons. These, Reagan argued, now needed modernising. The cost was very high in financial and social terms. The United States didn't have sufficient funds which meant that the poor would lose out – just as they had during the war when Johnson's Great Society programme was shelved.

America's three million veterans of the war would go on paying its cost long after the war was over. A Veterans Administration survey in 1988 estimated that some 500 000 veterans suffered from 'post-traumatic stress disorder'. Its symptoms could take ten or 15 years to appear. Depression, panic and rage attacks are features of the disorder. They are often followed by divorce, drug addiction, alcoholism and suicide.

B Americans at first tried to forget the Vietnam War. It wasn't until nearly ten years after the last American soldier left that a national monument was built. It's made of highly polished black granite. 150 000 people attended its opening.

Missing in action

One stumbling block in the way of better relations between the United States and Vietnam was the Missing-in-Action (MIA) issue. Rumours continued that some American servicemen were still prisoners of the communists. The United States refused to discuss **reparations** to Vietnam until the fates of all the MIAs were known. The Vietnamese wouldn't discuss MIAs until the Americans promised to pay reparations.

In November 1982 the veterans of the war finally got a national memorial in Washington. It was paid for by private donations. It lists the names of all those 58 132 men and eight women who died. Also recorded are 2413 others who are listed as Missing in Action. It is a dignified and moving monument and it was an important step for the United States in coming to terms with the war and the men who fought it.

The end

In 1985 an American veteran, William Ehrhart, went back to Vietnam. There he spoke to a North Vietnamese general.

'Would it have mattered if we had done things differently?' Ehrhart asked.

'No,' the general replied after a pause. 'Probably not. History was not on your side. We were fighting for our homeland. What were you fighting for?'

Ehrhart answered, 'Nothing that really mattered.'

C Not everyone liked the granite memorial to the war. Some wanted a more traditional symbol for the men who fought the war. In 1984 this bronze sculpture of three soldiers was unveiled.

Why did the United States lose the Vietnam War?

1 Why was the American army so keen to help John Wayne make The Green Berets?
2 How did Hollywood films after the war show a different view of Vietnam?
3 Can you suggest any reason why these films wouldn't have been made during the war?
4 In what ways were the American people still paying for the cost of the war in the 1980s?
5 Copy the chart below into your file under the title: 'Why did the United States lose the war?' Your task is to find evidence in the text to support each of the reasons in the left-hand column. The middle column indicates where you'll find some useful information. Once you have found the relevant evidence, complete the right-hand column. An example has been done for you.

Extended writing

'The United States lost the war in Vietnam because it did not use enough force.' What is your view of this interpretation? You should aim to write about 300 words or so. The following issues will help you:

- the numbers of troops sent to Vietnam;
- the bombing campaigns over North Vietnam, Laos, and Cambodia;
- American tactics against guerrilla warfare;
- American reluctance to use nuclear weapons;
- public opinion in the United States;
- morale of the American and communist forces.

You should think about how much force the Americans did use. Would more troops and more bombing have made any difference? Should they have used nuclear weapons? Were the political reasons for the United States' defeat more important than the military ones?

Reason for the defeat of the United States	Relevant chapter	I have found the following evidence to support this reason
The policies of the South Vietnamese and Americans were unpopular	Chapters 3, 4, 5	South Vietnamese governments failed to give land to the peasants; Diem's policies were anti-Buddhist; there was much corruption; 'strategic hamlets' programme was a failure.
The war was costing the United States too much	Chapters 13, 17	
American troops had low morale and motivation	Chapters 11, 17	
Public opinion became hostile to the war and forced the United States to withdraw	Chapters 10, 13	
China and the USSR provided vital military and economic aid to North Vietnam	Chapter 16	
VC and NVA tactics were more effective and their troops were more motivated.	Chapters 3, 7, 8	

Glossary

colony – a country under the control of another more powerful country (Vietnam was a colony of France until 1954)

Cold War – the state of tension (but not actual war) which existed between the Soviet Union and the United States from the late 1940s to the late 1980s

communist – someone who believes that the workers and peasants should control the country and that it should be free from foreign rule

Congress – the United States' equivalent of Britain's Parliament; Congress has to approve all the president's proposals before they can become law

conscription – the compulsory recruitment of men, and sometimes women, into the armed forces

coup d'état – commonly called a 'coup': the overthrow of the government by a small group of plotters, very often inside the army

domino theory – the idea that communism was spreading throughout South East Asia, each country falling to communism like a row of dominoes falling over. Each one that fell knocked the next one over, and so on

empire – a group of colonies under the control of another country

guerrilla – a type of soldier who uses hit-and-run tactics against the enemy and generally does not wear a uniform; these tactics are often used by weaker forces against a more powerful opponent in what is called a guerrilla war

Korean War 1950–53 – fought between communist North Korea (which was supported by communist China and the Soviet Union) and South Korea and its American allies

nationalist – someone who wants to free their country from foreign control and make it fully independent. Nationalists can also want to see their country dominate others

propaganda – methods used to persuade people to believe certain ideas or behave in a certain way; sometimes involves the use of deliberate lies

provenance – the provenance of a source is about who wrote it and when. Is there anything in the writer's background which makes his or her views more or less reliable? It is important for historians to know a source's provenance to help decide on its reliability and value

puppet – an individual or country controlled by another more powerful individual or country

reparations – compensation in money or goods for damage caused by one country to another. Vietnam demanded reparations from the United States

Supreme Court – the highest legal authority in the United States, consisting of nine judges

Vichy – the area of France in the Second World War controlled by French collaborators with the Germans

Index

Acknowledgements

The front cover shows US marines in Vietnam reproduced courtesy of Associated Press.

The Publishers would like to thank the following for permission to reproduce material in this volume:

Abacus for an extract from *Nam* by M Baker (1987); Appleton Century Crofts for an extract from *Documents of American History Vol. 2*, edited by H S Commager (1968); Facts on File for an extract from *The Vietnam War, An Eyewitness History* by S Wexler (1992); Granada Books for an extract from *If I Die in a Combat Zone* by T O'Brien (1980); HarperCollins for an extract from *The Vietnam Wars, 1945–1990* by M B Young, (1991); IB Tauris Publishers for an extract from *Vietnam – A Portrait of its People at War* by D Chanoff and D Van Thoai (1996); New York Times Magazine copyright © 1973 by the New York Times Company. Reprinted by permission. Pan Books for an extract from *Dispatches* by M Herr, (1978) and for an extract from *A Bright Shining Lie* by Neil Sheenan (1990); Century for an extract from *Vietnam – A History* by S Karnow, (1991); Presidio for an extract from *The American Infantryman in Vietnam* by J R Ebert (1993); Ramparts Press, San Francisco for an extract from *The Flower of the Dragon: The Breakdown of the US Army in Vietnam* by R Boyle (1972) quoted in *The Vietnam War, An Eyewitness History* by S Wexler (Facts on File, 1992); S M Hersh for an extract from *My Lai 4* by S M Hersh (1970) quoted in *The Bloody Game, An Anthology of Modern War* by P Fussel (Abacus, 1991); Salamander Books for an extract from *The Vietnam War* edited by R Bonds (1979).

The Publishers would also like to thank the following for permission to reproduce copyright illustrations in this volume:

Associated Press p.10, 13, 23, 31, 38; Australian War Memorial p.15; British Film Institute p.44; Colorific p.3; Corbis UK Ltd p. 5, 9, 14, 22, 26, 28, 32, 33, 34, 39, 45a, b; Fearing p.35; Hartford Times p.36; Katz Pictures p.11; Keystone p.42; Magnum p.16, 17, 18, 24, 29, 30; Popperphoto p.21; Punch p.37; Sov/East Photo p.12.

(**a** above; **b** below)

Every effort has been made to trace and acknowledge ownership of copyright. The Publishers will be glad to make suitable arrangements with any copyright owners whom it has not been possible to contact.

British Library Cataloguing in Publication Data
A catalogue record for this title is available from The British Library
ISBN 0–340–71125–6

First published in 1998
Impression number   10   9   8   7   6   5   4   3   2
Year   2002   2001   2000   1999

In memory of John Aylett, who devised this series.

Typeset by GreenGate Publishing Services, Tonbridge, Kent.

Printed for Hodder & Stoughton Educational, a division of Hodder Headline Plc, 338 Euston Road, London NW1 3BH by Cayfosa, Barcelona.